PRAISE FOR *BE THE ONE FOR KIDS*

"When you do what's right, you can change the world, and you can change the life of a child! *Be the One for Kids* is a wonderful, inspiring collection of experiences and practical opportunities that remind us to do what's right each and every day for kids. Join the movement and be the one!"

—**Hamish Brewer,** the relentless principal

"Do you want to be that teacher who students remember for a lifetime? *Be the One for Kids* will not only inspire and motivate but will give you practical ideas to take back to the schoolhouse to build unforgettable relationships with students, parents, colleagues, and community members."

—**Beth Houf,** proud principal and
coauthor of *Lead Like a Pirate*

"*Be the One for Kids*, by author Ryan Sheehy, is a powerful reminder for all of us about the importance of taking time to pause and enjoy the opportunities that we have been given to make a significant impact on all kids. This book will take you on a journey and challenge you to become a better educator so that you too can be that one person who our children not only deserve but, quite frankly, need in order to have the best chance for success."

—**Jimmy Casas,** senior fellow; International Center for
Leadership in Education, educator, author, and speaker

"In *Be the One for Kids*, Ryan has touched on the most powerful tool we have as educators and mentors . . . our ability to influence young people! After reading this book, you will believe for sure, that every kid needs a champion and advocate!"

—**Salome Thomas-EL,** award-winning principal,
speaker and author

"Ryan has created a masterpiece of motivation for educators by reminding us all of why we entered the profession. His insight on the simplicity of loving kids and loving what we do is inspiring and validating. It is a book that should be kept in sight, so it can serve as a quick reference through its focused chapters and will support our efforts to be the best we can be. Ryan's book is a must for all educators, no matter their title. Whether you are a novice or have years of experience, it will speak to your teacher heart. It has certainly made an imprint on mine."

—**Bethany Hill,** principal and lead learner at
Central Elementary, Cabot, Arkansas

"As a classroom teacher, education leader, and advocate for kids everywhere, I cannot give *Be the One for Kids* high enough praise. Ryan shares his personal stories, raw emotions, and experiences in relatable ways that make this book impossible to put down. You have the power inside you to change the world by helping all students feel successful, loved, and valued. This book serves as a guide for exactly how to do just that."

—**Kayla Delzer,** globally awarded teacher,
author, CEO: Top Dog Teaching, Inc.

"One moment, one smile, one interaction, or one person can make a difference in a child's life. In his book, *Be the One for Kids*, Ryan Sheehy shares stories, examples, and many great ideas to encourage and stimulate educators' thinking about how to be the one for kids every day. In small and large ways, we positively impact children, we inspire others, and we show compassion and kindness to all when we choose to be the one for kids."

—**Kas Nelson,** lead learner, Vici Elementary School, Oklahoma

"Every educator wants to be the one who makes a difference, but trying to do it all to ensure we make an impact can feel completely overwhelming. In *Be the One for Kids*, Ryan Sheehy provides an inspirational and practical plan that will equip educators to truly change students' lives."

—**Aaron Hogan,** author of *Shattering the Perfect Teacher Myth*

"This book is not just for teachers and administrators. This book is for all those who work at a school site, who have the power to be the one not only for students but to colleagues, parents, and the community! If we each do our part in being the one, our classrooms, schools, districts, and communities will be forever changed in huge and positive ways!"

—**Jessica Gomez,** principal

"Ryan Sheehy weaves stories from growing up through his experiences as an educator and administrator to illustrate how we can all be the one for our students. As a seasoned educator and veteran principal, Ryan's suggestions and ideas make me want to be a better leader."

—**Mark French,** principal, Gatewood Elementary, Hopkins, Minnesota; past president of Minnesota Elementary School Principals' Association; 2015 Minnesota National Distinguished Principal

"Ryan Sheehy crushes it with his first book *Be the One for Kids* Not only is this relevant for all educators *now,* it will be a go-to guide for the next twenty years! So many quick and easy takeaways to help you and your friends, colleagues, or staff make an immediate impact on #AllKids, right now!"

—**Jeff Kubiak,** disrupter, advocate for #AllKids, elementary educator

"Some books teach you information; others challenge your thinking. After reading *Be the One for Kids*, I'm left inspired not only to be 'The One' for kids but to inspire others to be 'The One' our future generation needs. More than a book, this is a movement. Ryan places a call to action, gives practical advice, and challenges us all to be 'The One' who can bring change. Crafted with honesty and passion, this book will have educators reflect on their current impact and how they can be a greater influence for our students."

—Lynmara Colon, principal

"*Be the One for Kids* is a true gift of messages for educators from someone who is in the trenches with the rest of us. Ryan Sheehy has done a great job in compiling a series of short quips that remind & inspire us all of the important words, actions, and mindsets that really make a difference every day. The book is filled with inspiring ideas that are immediately actionable to help build and improve school and/or classroom culture! I will start implementing these strategies tomorrow!"

—Eric J. Chagala, EdD, principal, Vista Innovation and Design Academy (VIDA)

"*Be the One for Kids* is a motivating call to action for all educators and a challenge to reflect on the numerous ways we can support kids. Ryan shares personal experiences and lessons learned to point out how we all have the power to be the one for kids; we just have to reflect and be intentional about it. I was challenged and motivated, after reading this book, to refocus my own work and be the one for kids, and I believe this is a must-read for any and all educators!"

—Jonathan Eagan, assistant superintendent

"*Be the One for Kids* is an inspirational guide to creating better schools as Ryan Sheehy captures the essence of servant leadership and perfectly illustrates how to become more intentional when working with kids. Most importantly, this book is a subtle reminder that every single day is a new opportunity to build a school culture that permeates joy, happiness and unconditional love for others. Now, more than ever, we need educators that will put kids first and lead the way with smiles, hugs, and high fives. Be the one to make it happen!"

—**Dr. Greg Goins**, director of educational leadership/professor of education at Georgetown College (Kentucky), former school superintendent

"From morning greetings to connecting with other educators, this book will inspire you to #BeTheOne for your students. Reading this will help you remember what gets you up every morning, who you look forward to seeing every day, and how you can make a difference in the lives of those around you."

—**Jessica Cabeen**, @JessicaCabeen, author and 2017 Minnesota National Distinguished Principal

"Sheehy's *Be the One for Kids* is filled with the heart, soul, and guts of a reflective educator and, most importantly, a human being who advocates for students with a 100 percent commitment to them without any hesitation, whatsoever. This amazing book is filled with a brilliant forty-eight chapter thought map about how we can 'be the one' to stand up for and fight for our students each day. *Be the One for Kids* will get your juices flowing and provide you with a B12 shot for spreading the joy of how we can change students' lives with every tick of the clock."

—**Rick Jetter**, PhD, author of multiple books including *Escaping the School Leader's Dunk Tank* and *Let Them Speak!*, cofounder of Pushing Boundaries Consulting, LLC.

"You can read this book in one sitting, but I challenge you not to! Take your time as you read, reflect on the stories, and consider how each idea fits your leadership role. The ideas in the book might seem simple, yet I would argue the implementation of each is career changing. If you work these ideas into your leadership style, you will create a school parents will beg to get their children into!"

—**Phil Boyte,** school culture consultant,
author *School Culture by Design*

"Ryan Sheehy's new book, *Be the One For Kids*, is a virtual cover-to-cover celebration brought to life by a lovely patchwork of real life stories that honor educators, parents, and children. Each page is Ryan's heartfelt plea for each of us to rise to the occasion and be the one for kids and for each other. Every personalized story reminds us why we became educators while his forty-seven 'Be the One' testaments will help us to re-envision schools as safe and supportive spaces where respectful collaborations will become embedded in our school culture. I can imagine a 'Be the One' movement just beyond the horizon as educators everywhere enthusiastically commit to showing up in the name of children."

—**Dr. Mary Howard**, education consultant and author

"*Be the One for Kids* is a true reflection of what a leader should be and should exhibit, as Ryan takes an inside look into the real world of the principalship. It is an easy read with points to consider and share to spread the notion of being the one for kids, while inspiring every educator to be the person who every child deserves."

—**Barry Richburg**, principal, Yates Mill
Elementary School, Raleigh, North Carolina

"It's time to step up! In *Be the One for Kids*, Ryan is transparent about his experiences and is candid about why and how, as educators, we are obligated to be the one because relationships matter most. His heartfelt recollection reminds us that, when we choose this profession, we are in fact choosing to be the model for kids—to be there to lift them up, support them, acknowledge them, and encourage them—no matter where we are on our journey as educators: classroom teacher, coach, or administrator, *Be the One for Kids* is just what we all need to remind us of our why—why we chose this profession— because we wanted to make a difference and each one of us is a difference-maker."

—**Onica L. Mayers**, @O_L_Mayers, lead learner,
Principal of the Year 2017

"*Be the One for Kids* is a call to action for all educators to engage, support, challenge, inspire, and uplift each and every student in our schools and classrooms. *Be the One for Kids* challenges educators to be focused change agents who remember their 'why.' Ryan articulates a clear message that it's time to be relentless in doing our best for kids . . . all kids . . . all the time . . . no matter what. It's a powerful message that needs to be read, shared, and lived in our school communities!"

—**Mandy Ellis,** principal

"*Be the One for Kids* shares a variety of situations that all educators face at some point in their careers. Ryan's personal stories for each situation bring you face to face with a real-life connection. The thoughtful questions to end each chapter, with a challenge to Tweet a response, are the things of all good Twitter chats. Upon reading each chapter, you will be encouraged to be the one for kids."

—**Jay Posick,** principal,
Merton Intermediate School,
Merton, Wisconsin

BE THE

ONE

FOR KIDS

YOU HAVE THE POWER TO
CHANGE THE LIFE OF A CHILD

RYAN SHEEHY

Published by Dave Burgess Consulting, Inc.
San Diego, CA
DaveBurgessConsulting.com

Cover Design by Genesis Kohler
Editing and Interior Design by My Writers' Connection

Library of Congress Control Number: 2018933186
Paperback ISBN: 978-1-946444-63-9
Ebook ISBN: 978-1-946444-64-6

First Printing: March 2018

DEDICATION

This book is dedicated to all educators out there who are bringing it each day for kids. You are my inspiration and living proof that we all have power to Be the One for Kids.

To my wife, Barbara, thank you for being my daily support system. To my kids, Robert, Joshua, Julianna, and Zachary, thank you for being the reason I get up each day and try to change the world.

BELIEVE IN
THEM.
#BETHEONE

CONTENTS

CULTURE

CREATIVITY

EMPOWERMENT

CONTINUED LEARNING

LIVE YOUR PASSION

#BETHEONE

FOREWORD

BY ADAM WELCOME, AUTHOR/SPEAKER/EDUCATOR

People don't choose a career in education for the money. Educators want to make a difference, to impact lives, to encourage, to spread a message that will help shape future generations for many years to come. People choose education to Be the One for their students!

There have been a few times in my life where I've been silent, where I've turned my head and didn't speak up, and those are all times I regret. In the moment, it seemed something wasn't right, and for reasons I can't explain, I didn't stand up; I didn't speak up. I wasn't there for my students, my colleagues, or even myself.

I promise you now that it is all very clear to me. I'm going to be an upstander! Bystanders won't fight for kids who have learning disabilities, speak another language, or have nobody in their lives rooting for them or for those kids that just don't believe in themselves. Upstanders will!

When we became educators, we all took an oath that we would support, build, nourish, push, guide, and do absolutely whatever it takes to ensure all our students succeed. As we all know, our kids deserve it, and we must be the encourager in chief!

Be the One for Kids is a call to action; it's a movement; it's a rallying cry for all adults who work with children to not look around, to not look for an excuse, to not point the finger and say, "not me." It's for you to realize you have the power. You have the power to change the life of a child—with your words, your actions, and your belief that YOU have what it takes inside to push forward, and that our students do too!

We must celebrate *all* achievements; nothing can go unnoticed. We must offer unwavering support for our students. When others say they won't, they can't, they shouldn't, or that they never will, we must more than ever stand up and say, "I will Be the One!"

Dear student: I will stand in front of you, next to you, and behind you. I'll guide you on your educational journey. I promise I will. There may be others fighting for you as well, but know that I'm 100 percent committed.

I'm committed to being an upstander and telling anyone who will listen about all the bright spots, all the magic moments, and all the wins we celebrate and see every day with our students.

Who's with me?!

Introduction

For the past thirteen years, I have taught at twelve different schools—elementary, middle, and high school—and have served as an administrator at two others. Those schools were some of the poorest and wealthiest schools in California, and they all held one thing in common: Within all of them, there were educators who admitted to being afraid of doing something different or unique because they might be the only one to try it. Too often when educators take a risk and do something different, they are put under a magnifying glass, decisions are scrutinized, and intentions are questioned. That is why it is so important to understand what we are doing and why we are doing it.

After speaking with educators around the world, I believe this to be the case at most schools. For nine years, I was a physical education teacher with a passion for challenging the status quo in education. I was challenged and questioned but was determined to change the perception of a physical educator. I made every decision around what was best for kids, and I was ready to explain to those who questioned me why I was doing things.

Having gained unique insights after experiencing life at many different schools, I decided to compile a book of my thoughts and experiences. I want to show others that one person can make the difference in a child's life and in a student's success. I want all educators, parents, coaches, and everyone in between to know they have power to *Be the One for Kids*.

Throughout these chapters, readers will experience stories from my personal life, my life as a teacher, and my journey as an administrator. Readers will experience the daily emotions that are real in our kids' lives and will see my soul come to life on the pages.

This book will challenge you to become a better person and will take you on a journey that shows how you can enhance your teaching practices by simply building relationships with students, parents, colleagues, and community members. Our education system isn't perfect, but it's at its best when every educator is unleashing their power to Be the One for Kids.

CULTURE

— 1 —

BE THE ONE FOR
THE MOVEMENT

Most people go into education because they want to make a
difference. It isn't money, fame, or recognition educators
seek; it's the chance to leave a legacy in the heart of a child. My bet
is that *you* became an educator because you want to make a difference. You are in the right field. Education is a career that enables
you to make an impact on future generations by changing the lives
of young people in the present.

Be the One for Kids came from many different conversations
with educators from a variety of schools. In the past thirteen years,
I have taught at twelve schools (some years I taught at six different elementary schools per week) and was a vice principal for two
years at a high school before becoming an elementary principal. My
journey to becoming a principal was very purposeful and a huge
learning experience. The journey was tough but well worth it. I am
at a point where I love my job. I wake up each day and spend time
with teachers, parents, and students. Having taught at every level
in education and at many different sites in different socioeconomic
areas, I have seen what works as well as what needs to change.

I want to share my passion for education and my passion for
relationships, and I believe educators can be the one for kids by simply enhancing their teaching practices and building relationships.

Throughout my journey, I have had countless conversations with educators who were filled with excuses. They chose not to try something new because no one else would try it. Too afraid to make the leap or intimidated because it was not the popular thing, they let opportunity pass them by. Experience has shown that sometimes all it takes is one person willing to take a risk and get creative to bring about positive change. I have had the privilege of seeing firsthand how one person willing to make a different choice can change the life of a child.

Not every child inherently loves school. I had the pleasure to teach with an educator who took that to heart. She felt it was her job to make sure every student not only left her class with all first-grade content knowledge but also found something they loved about school. She was determined to find that one thing that would get kids out of bed.

Working with the local high school wood shop class, she was able to create the opportunity for first-grade students to have wood-shop woven into their daily curriculum. Fast forward twelve years: Graduating from high school, these students came back to thank this educator for helping them find that one thing that ignited their passion for education.

You possess the power to Be the One for Kids. Don't be afraid to unleash it.

THINGS TO CONSIDER AND TWEET

1. How can you Be the One for Kids?
2. How can you Be the One for Others?
3. How do you find that one thing that ignites their passion for learning?

#BETHEONE

2

BE THE ONE WHO KNOWS KIDS' STORIES

Who is that student in your class that challenges you? Who is that student you can't get out of your mind? What is his or her story? How are you going to help him or her succeed? How are you helping them unleash their potential?

When I was a second grader at Olive Elementary School in Vista, California, it was a year-round school, and I was on the green track. One of the months we were off track, our home phone rang, and it was my teacher, Mrs. Lewis. She invited me to have pizza with her and a few other students, and I was over-the-moon excited! Throughout this trip to my classroom, she asked us all about our lives. She wanted to know what we did outside of school, how we spent our free time, and what our families were like. She wanted to know my story, and that was an amazing feeling.

The experience made a strong impression on me, and today I strive to be like Mrs. Lewis and to know my own students' stories. Every single individual who walks into our school buildings has a story. When we learn those stories, we are more able to provide the tools our students need to succeed.

Think back to your own childhood. Which teacher learned your story? How did it make you feel?

All children deserve to have someone who invests time in them and learns about their lives. That investment also has the potential to pay out major dividends over time.

Spending time in high school as a teacher and as a vice principal showed me firsthand the power of building relationships with students. One year, during the first week of school, a girl came into the office kicking and screaming. She had been about to fight another student but was stopped right before contact was made. She was loud and out of control and was placed in my office to blow off steam. After letting her sit for about twenty minutes, I started a conversation. I looked her in the eyes and said, "Tell me about yourself."

She had quite the story. This student was in the foster system. Her father had been killed when she was little, and her mother was in jail. She had been abused and continued to bounce from foster home to foster home.

For the next two years, we started each day together in my office. She would catch me up on her life, different things that were happening, things that were troubling her, and what her dreams were. That initial conversation in the wake of her meltdown sparked an important relationship. Today I occasionally get messages from her, and one of the most recent said she had graduated and was excited to be starting college in the fall. In the note, she thanked me for believing in her and taking the time to know her story.

When educators invest the time to learn their students' stories, they have a better understanding of what motivates them. With that knowledge, it becomes easier to empower a student to succeed. Never give up the opportunity to have a conversation that might build a relationship with a student at your school.

The next time you have a free moment to engage a student, try asking about family or sports or favorite music or college plans.

Afterward, reflect on that experience and see if the interaction establishes a new relationship, improves an existing one, or has a significant effect on the students' outlook at school.

Know your students' stories, and you just might build relationships that last a lifetime.

THINGS TO CONSIDER AND TWEET ————————————

1. When is the last time you stopped and learned someone's story?
2. Who learned your story?
3. How did someone learning your story change you?

————————————— #BETHEONE

BE THE SPARK FOR
SOMEONE TODAY.
{ **#BETHEONE** }

3

BE THE ONE WHO MAKES KIDS FEEL SPECIAL

High school is a time when students begin to figure out who they are. Some students enter with a good sense of self, while others really struggle with the process. Freshman year, for me, was tough. I transferred from a private school into the local public high school. I went from fifteen total kids in my grade to 350 students in my grade. It was a big jump.

As I made the transition and worked on getting to know others, there was a teacher who made me feel special. I can still remember sitting in the PE office, talking with the teachers while others were getting dressed out. On this particular day, a yearbook photographer wanted to get a picture of the PE teacher for the yearbook. The teacher thought it would be funny to put me in a headlock for the pic. For some reason, this fun interaction has stuck with me for years, as it is one of my favorite pictures from high school. It made me feel special.

What makes you feel special?

What makes you smile?

What makes you feel appreciated?

Maybe it's a verbal acknowledgement of your efforts or a polite inquiry about how you are feeling. Now think about your students. How can you foster those same feelings of appreciation in the classroom? I believe the answer is modeling. We must model that kind of behavior daily, teaching students how to give and accept praise, and showing them how it can make others feel good about themselves.

When working in a school setting, it's imperative to look for the good in every situation and for ways to provide positive feedback to students and coworkers. It's especially helpful when schools have some official way to acknowledge kids for making the correct choice and going above and beyond in good deeds. We need to do this for the adults in our lives as well.

When my kids do something remarkable or outstanding, I call their homes. I bring the student into my office, we make the call, and you should see their faces light up when I sing their praises to their parents. Kids inherently want to impress the adults in their lives. After the phone call, I continue the conversation with the student, and we wrap up with a selfie that I print out for them to take home. When they leave school that day, I know they feel special.

Every month at our school we concentrate on a character trait, and the month culminates with student recognition. This year we added in a staff member and teacher who would be recognized. It was great to see these adults get excited when they realized their colleagues had noticed and rewarded their behaviors—and especially important for our students to witness.

We live in a society that constantly focuses on the negative. Educators must continually fight against that tendency, making sure their schools are places where the focus is on positive progress. The next time you walk into your school, resolve to Be the One who makes the children and adults in your path feel special and supported.

THINGS TO CONSIDER AND TWEET ━━━━━━━━━━━━━━━

1. How do you make students feel special?
2. How do you make other staff members feel good about themselves?
3. How does recognition and acknowledgement affect school culture?

━━━━━━━━━━━━━━━━━━━━━ #BETHEONE

GET OUTSIDE AND HAVE FUN WITH KIDS.

#BETHEONE

4

BE THE ONE WHO SAYS YES

Is it okay if I try something new? Yes!

May I purchase some new technology for coding? Yes!

May I attend this conference? Yes!

It feels amazing to say *yes* to educators. Obviously, the answer can't always be yes, but rather than saying *no* in those cases, we must focus on finding alternative solutions—a happy compromise. The goal is to empower educators to enhance their teaching practices, which means saying yes as often as possible. And the payoff for encouraging educators to take the leap and try something new is that others will follow. Be that person who never stops growing or helping their colleagues grow as well.

Let's face it—schools must grow with the times. When teachers, principals, and other school leaders do this, they are putting students first. For so long, school leaders and district officials have been telling their educators, "Sorry, that is a great idea, but we do not have funding." Enough! Our children cannot afford for us to make any more excuses, and all educators must deliver our best, each and every day.

We must take time to develop as educators to make sure we are teaching skills that will be relevant, necessary, and in-demand during the years to come. If we make learning relevant, students will be engaged and stay engaged.

Over the past few years, I have been able to say yes frequently. Teachers and parents were shocked, at first, but now know to expect it. I must admit—I probably said yes to some things I would say no to today. Not everything was thought out the way I would have liked. Saying yes, however, has created a culture in which teachers are more comfortable stepping out of their comfort zones and trying something new.

A kindergarten team that had been demoralized by hearing the word no or "we can't try that" has been able to grow exponentially because they have been empowered to say yes to themselves and to their students. Things in the past they were afraid to try and needed to be walked through are now being done on a consistent basis and are used as a way to showcase things in their classrooms. Teachers who had been adamant about not using any technology in their classrooms are asking for technology and help with implementing it. They saw the power that technology was having in other classrooms and wanted their students to have those skills as well. They have come to see it as a helpful tool and not just a time filler. Never stop being willing to try something new. Because these educators are saying yes to their students and to themselves, they have been able to unleash opportunities for their students that would not have been there.

Be the One Who Says Yes.

THINGS TO CONSIDER AND TWEET ━━━━━━━━━━━━━━━━━

1. How often do you say yes?
2. What has saying yes done for your students?
3. If the answer has to be no, how do you problem solve?

━━━━━━━━━━━━━━━━━━━━━━━━ #BETHEONE

— 5 —

BE THE ONE WHO GREETS PEOPLE ON CAMPUS

I walked into an educator conference session and was immediately greeted with a fist bump and a welcome. The room buzzed with purpose as the presenter established an environment where people wanted to be and wanted to learn.

People like happy places and enjoy being welcome and having their presence appreciated. As an educator, you have the opportunity to set the tone each day and Be the One who creates a positive vibe in your school building throughout the day.

Here are some easy ways to create an amazing environment where students and educators can learn alongside one another:

1. GIVE FIST BUMPS AND HIGH FIVES.

As kids enter your building, greet them with some flair. Educators who do this well make a point of telling students they love fist bumps and high fives. Each morning, whether you are in a high school or elementary school, you can watch students' faces light up with a welcome.

2. GET YOUR MASCOT ON.

Putting on a mascot costume every once in a while can make so many positive impacts on your campus. High school students flock to the mascot to take selfies, and in elementary, school the parents line up for that one picture of their child with the school mascot.

Happy students make better learners, so take a risk and try something different.

3. PLAY SOME MUSIC.

Music taps into our creative side and makes the mornings fun. Blasting music also wakes up the neighborhood and makes families' walks to school a little livelier. Enlisting the help of a DJ to start the school year off right is a great investment. You can use music to create the environment that is wanted at every school.

4. RIDE THE BUS.

When you have the opportunity to ride the bus, do it. You should see our students' faces when they get on the bus and see an educator sitting there. Take the time and build the relationships with students and the bus driver. Too often we only know our students in the classroom and in school. Take the time to see what happens on the bus, and you will see the dividends immediately.

5. GET A LITTLE SILLY.

Don't take yourself so seriously. Show that you are vulnerable and willing to have fun. Kids need to see us loving our jobs. Without that, who would ever want to work in education? Any time our parents' club wants to do something outrageous—like turning me into an ice-cream sundae or pelting me with whip cream pies—I say yes. Through the years, I have heard some folks say students shouldn't be able to do that to an adult on campus, but I disagree. Not only is it all in good fun, it creates a culture no one wants to leave. We need to change the way educators are viewed. We are all part of the team, no matter our title.

THINGS TO CONSIDER AND TWEET ━━━━━━━━━━━━━━

1. How do you greet students when they arrive at school each day?

2. How would you describe the environment on your campus?

3. When is the last time you left your classroom or office to hang out with kids? What did you do?

━━━━━━━━━━━━━━━━━━━━━ **#BETHEONE**

KIDS DESERVE GREATNESS.

BE GREAT TODAY.

#BETHEONE

6

BE THE ONE WHO
MAKES AN IMPACT

how up each day, and bring it for kids!

When students arrive at school each morning, we don't know what has happened since the last time they left our classrooms. Even in the most affluent of areas, kids can experience great turmoil at home.

A few years ago, I worked with a first-grade teacher who was amazing. She would greet her students at the door each day with an extreme amount of love and compassion. She genuinely cared for each one of the students. At the time, the neighborhood was going through a transition, and kids were coming from all different types of homes. The school was Title I, and it was difficult to get a lot of things done due to red tape. This teacher could have had a job at any school she wanted, and I wondered why she had chosen our school.

One fall morning as I arrived on campus at 7:45 a.m., I noticed something different in the air, a feeling of uneasiness. As I continued to walk across campus, I was shocked to see some of our students and their families hiding in the bushes. I looked at one of the mothers, and when our eyes connected, I could see how genuinely scared she was of being found. Without saying a word, she asked me to keep walking and not to draw any attention to her and her family. I continued to walk.

My classroom was next door to that amazing first-grade teacher. I stopped in to tell her what I just witnessed. She abruptly stopped me and asked, "Do you know why they were hiding?" I told her I was unsure, and she began to cry. It turned out police raided the three apartment complexes surrounding the school, and those families were scared of being deported. It was a common fear among our parent community when law enforcement came around.

Sometime later I met up with the first-grade teacher again and told her I felt my emotions had gotten the best of me that day. I was shocked and saddened at the fear on those families' faces. She sat me down, looked right into my eyes and told me to have faith in the positive impact I was having on my students. "Know that you are helping these kids more than any of them could ever admit. They care about you. They look up to you. They want to be you. That is why I have never left this school, and that is why I bring my very best, each and every day."

I left the room filled with emotion, a little unsure how to feel or respond. I realized that my students needed me more than I had ever thought. I provided security, safety, and a sense of normalcy.

For some of our students, these are the most important things in their lives. Every day, educators around the world are making an extreme impact on students, but in reality, students are leaving their mark on us. Be the One who knows your impact, and don't be afraid of learning from them.

THINGS TO CONSIDER AND TWEET

1. In what areas do you make the biggest impact on students?
2. How can teachers stay mindful of the impact they make on students?

#BETHEONE

7

BE THE ONE WHO SHOWS KIDS HOW TO HAVE FUN

What do you do to have fun?

How do you model fun at school?

No matter the activity, we need to find the fun in it. Educators are constantly looking for interesting, engaging, and fun ways to make the learning experience more enjoyable. Teachers, administrators, and other staff members should have smiles on their faces every day they're at school. We need to model fun for our students and show them we love being educators. Here are a few ways educators can show having fun at school:

1. DON'T BE AFRAID TO DRESS UP.

Every school has spirit days and other days where educators and students can dress up. When educators walk around in a costume, they grow more comfortable with having fun and doing wild things. As soon as kids see you walking around in costume, they get huge smiles on their faces. High school students still go crazy for spirit days and love seeing school staff dressed up.

2. WHEN YOU WORK WITH KIDS, KNOW WHAT KIDS LIKE TO DO FOR FUN.

Whether you are a principal, teacher, or everything in between, it's okay to have fun. Educators' roles are constantly changing, and it is a good thing. Every year our educators are being pied in the face, turned into an ice cream sundae, put in a dunk tank, and duct taped to a wall.

Why would anyone do any of this?

Because it's fun. These activities make everyone laugh, relax, and enjoy some time away from their normal routine. It also shows educators' personalities in a different light. Some people think kids should never see adults letting off steam. Kids disagree.

How will they understand it's okay to cut loose and have fun or to celebrate a victory if they never see us doing it?

3. SLIDE.

If you have never barreled down a slide with kids, you must! You will never forget the faces and comments the first time you do it. Everyone will be in awe of you climbing up that ladder, and everyone will want to watch. So get out there and start sliding with kids. If you work in a secondary school, and there is no slide, get creative—DJ at lunchtime in the cafeteria—and start a new tradition.

4. RIDE TRICYCLES AND SCOOTERS.

Kindergarteners love riding tricycles and scooters. When educators join in and ride the scooters, it's a blast—for themselves as well as the students. Adults who drop everything and go for a ride show students we are never too old or too overdressed to have fun.

5. READ TO A CLASS.

Educators who visit other classrooms to read a book aloud will see everyone overcome with joy and excitement. High school teachers who read aloud to their students are always shocked to see how much joy there is in their eyes. Take the opportunity to read to your own students, and don't be afraid to read to other classes as well.

6. RECESS.

Educators have vital roles in every school building. They command respect and expect students to follow school rules. Playing at recess with students isn't just an opportunity to have fun; it helps builds relationships with kids. Many high school and middle school educators who play sports with their students at lunch have reported an increased effectiveness in the classroom.

7. BE PRESENT.

Educators can look for opportunities to build on your relationships with kids and engage them in stimulating conversations. Being present means we need to have no distraction and have sincere conversations.

8. INTERACT.

Seek out opportunities to interact with students. Create lessons and design your day in a way that you can actually participate with and work alongside your students.

9. BE ACTIVE IN THE COMMUNITY.

School communities and the larger community tend to have many different events. The more events you can attend and in which you can build rapport, the better off you will be. Making time to attend these events will show families you are invested in their children.

10. PLAY MUSIC.

Music brings people together. It makes them happy. Nothing sets a pleasant tone for students, parents, teachers, and administrators like playing music as everyone walks onto campus in the morning. Families can hear the music from blocks away, and by the time they arrive, some folks are dancing. Some days there's even a dance party next to the speaker.

THINGS TO CONSIDER AND TWEET ━━━━━━━━━━━━━━━

1. What do you do at school to have fun?
2. How do you show students that being an educator is fun?
3. How do you allow your students and the rest of your school community to have fun with you?

━━━━━━━━━━━━━━━━━━━━━ #BETHEONE

8

BE THE ONE WHO ADVOCATES

When my wife was in second grade, her teacher told her she was dumb and would never read. After this encounter with her teacher, she ran home to tell her mom what had happened. When my wife tells the story, she describes in detail her mom's fierce facial expressions as she learned what the teacher had said. The next day, her mom hurried into school and demanded a classroom change. The change occurred, and my wife grew into a voracious reader who has a love of classic literature. In that circumstance, she needed an advocate, and the advocate was her mother.

Educators often deal with parents who don't always view their children with a great deal of patience or compassion or understanding.

Why does my child act this way?

Why is he such a pain?

Why is he so annoying?

These are actually some of the questions parents ask me, and it always makes me a little sad. They're kids! They're not fully formed, they're still learning how to behave, and they need someone in their corner. Kids need advocates who believe in them. My wife needed an advocate in second grade, and maybe it should have been her teacher, but it definitely turned out to be her mom.

Years ago, walking down the halls of the high school where I was a vice principal, I popped my head into a ceramics classroom where they happened to be taking a test. This class had been chosen to be an inclusion classroom where general education students worked alongside students who were severely handicapped. Scanning the room, I noticed a boy named Jose helping a student with special needs. The teacher didn't see what he was doing but heard him talking to another student. She rushed over to Jose, grabbed his test, and told him his test would be scored a zero for cheating. I quickly stepped in. Jose hadn't done anything but care for a student who needed assistance. He needed an advocate to intervene on his behalf. After some explanation, his teacher let him finish the test, and the class continued.

Too often I find myself being the one advocating for kids when they also need their parents and teachers to speak up for them. We must advocate for our kids. Kids need you to always believe in them and fight for what's best for them. Together we can create an education system that will take all students to the next level and make everyone succeed.

THINGS TO CONSIDER AND TWEET ━━━━━━━━━━━━━━━

1. How do you advocate for kids?
2. What has been the biggest challenge when advocating for your students?

━━━━━━━━━━━━━━━━━━━━━━━━━━ #BETHEONE

9

BE THE ONE WHO WELCOMES EVERYONE

Dontrell was a fifth grader who had transferred to our school from his nineteenth school in five years. His education was not consistent—much like his living conditions. He had spent his life bouncing around and not sure where he would be the next day. To arrive at school on time, he would get up at 5:30 a.m. and catch a train and then catch a bus to arrive at 8 a.m. From the start, he was at a disadvantage from our other students, but that did not stop him from having a positive attitude.

Upon his arrival, teachers and staff welcomed this student and learned who he was. Due to his family situation, he would spend much time in the front office after school. Not only was this child smart, but he had a wit about him much beyond his years, and everyone loved talking with him. Those conversations with him were rejuvenating for everyone. He came to this school for a new beginning, and he wasn't sure what was to come of it. He had faced much adversity and had come out stronger and more resilient. Transitioning to many schools at a young age is not easy, and it takes a toll on a child. Welcoming him into the school every day was the only way to help him feel comfortable in being there.

One of the best things about education is that every day is a brand-new start for everyone. No matter what happened the previous day, you are welcomed into the school buildings like it is the first day of the year.

How do you welcome your students daily?

How do you welcome your colleagues daily?

How do you welcome your families daily?

Reflecting on these three questions helps make sure we are making the start of each day as magical as day one. Not everyone in our buildings has the same story or even similar stories, but they deserve to have a fresh start daily.

THINGS TO CONSIDER AND TWEET

1. How do you ensure you welcome everyone daily?
2. How do your students feel when you arrive?
3. What are three new ways you can welcome students to your classroom or school?

#BETHEONE

10

BE THE ONE WHO WILL NOT TAKE NO FOR AN ANSWER

It was the final round of a vice principal interview. I got called into the boardroom where there were two directors, three principals, and the assistant superintendent of human resources. The role playing began immediately. An extremely upset parent demanded many things. I had just suspended their child for fighting, and supposedly it was provoked. I went into problem solving mode and calmed the parent down and began to build rapport. The role play came to an end, and the interview questions began. The interview lasted about an hour, then I headed home. I was interviewing for a vice principal position of a local high school.

Before I made it home, the assistant superintendent of human resources called and let me know that I would be meeting with the superintendent and the cabinet the next morning. I was over-the-moon excited, and I could barely sleep that night. The interview came, and I walked into a large room that had a large desk on one side, and on the other side were a few couches and chairs. The superintendent and the cabinet began their questioning. About halfway through the interview, the superintendent paused and asked if they could be honest with me. I responded, "Of course." He started with "Ryan, I am going to be honest. You are a physical education teacher, and I don't view PE teachers as instructional leaders." I made my case against it, but I was definitely shocked at what they had said. The interview wrapped up, and I headed home. I couldn't shake the feeling of having been treated like that.

Later that night, I got the call that the position had gone to someone else. Although it didn't surprise me, I still was not happy. It hurt. I had done so many different things to show everyone I was an instructional leader, and still the superintendent felt that because of the subject I taught, I was not an instructional leader.

I knew I had to do something different. I was given the answer of no, but I was not going to stop short of my dreams. I decided that if the leader of that district felt certain subject matter teachers could not be instructional leaders, then I didn't want to work in that environment. I wanted to work in a place that valued all their kids and all their staff, no matter their background. I decided to leave the district and take an administrator position in a district that valued all their people.

I challenge you to remember who you are and how you become who you are—and never take no for an answer on your dreams.

THINGS TO CONSIDER AND TWEET

1. Describe a time when you refused to take no for an answer.
2. How did that affect your interaction with students? When you can't or don't want to say yes to a student, how do you handle it?

#BETHEONE

— 11 —

BE THE ONE WHO DOESN'T LIMIT LEARNING

A t a meeting to welcome back my school staff, two of the items we covered were Google Classroom and how to build a class website. As I presented on Google classroom, I looked around the room and saw many faces similar to those of students when they are taught something for the first time: There were many blank stares and confused faces. That year was the first time we were using both of those platforms school wide. One was new for me, and the other I had experience using.

When you learn something new and are forced to teach others, you suddenly become the expert in the room. It's not always the easiest role to have. Many of our teachers were frustrated by having to learn a new application in such a short time. I pointed out that this is often how our students feel when there is a new lesson being presented in the classroom. After seeing our teachers' faces, it was clear some re-teaching was necessary. Time was short, so I knew I had to get creative. A few hours after talking with the staff, I decided to create a video using screencast techniques to methodically walk staff through the new program. Creating videos is an effective way to re-teach concepts in the classroom and can be utilized with teaching new concepts and ideas to other educators. Time is limited, so we are forced to get creative to make sure everyone is still on board. Facilitating re-teaching opportunities can be scary for professionals who have never used these platforms. Step outside your comfort zone and learn different techniques, then share those techniques with others. The sharing and learning of techniques drives everyone forward, making educators better for their students.

Create opportunities where students—and teachers—can learn whenever they are ready and wherever they are. Sometimes we go too fast and need to create opportunities for everyone to catch up. Don't let time, budget, or variety of learning levels limit the learning that goes on in our buildings daily.

THINGS TO CONSIDER AND TWEET

1. How do you create opportunities for enhanced learning at your school or in your classroom?
2. What are some new skills, programs or applications you have taken the time to learn this school year?

#BETHEONE

12

BE THE ONE WHO ENGAGES PARENTS

During a district-wide retreat, our superintendent gave a presentation, and while she was talking, a photo of a first-grade class flashed across the screen. There she was, my daughter. At the sight of her face, my mood instantly improved, and I sat up in my seat. As a parent of four children, there is nothing I love more than seeing my kids. Every time I take out my phone and see their photos, the endorphins go to work, and I can't stop smiling. If that happens to me, it happens to other parents too. That common ground gives educators the power to connect with the parents in their school community.

One of my goals as an educator is for parents to be involved in their child's educational experience. When parents pick up their kids at school, they should be able to ask about an activity in which they know their child participated that day. Use social media to open a window into the classroom. This lets everyone see what is happening daily and allows for these carpool conversations with parents and children. The communication is real and live, and you are showcasing your students and engaging your parents.

Another goal is to bring parents together to learn about how to better support their children's learning. Modeled after the popular EdCamp, a parent EdCamp is an extremely effective way to have a real-time conversation about a variety of topics about which they are concerned, such as special education, homework, nutrition, coding, computer science, science, writing, and literacy. Every month I create a YouTube video of me reading a book to students, and it's sent via email to our families. The purpose of the video is to encourage parent-child communication about the book and literacy in general.

Some of our families cannot afford computers or an Internet connection, so we started allowing students to take technology home. Every Friday, students line up in the office to check out different devices. The most popular item is the Sphero. Students are taking them home and coding with parents, which gives Mom and Dad a chance to be part of the learning process.

With our busier, harder-to-reach parents, we have taken a different approach. We established a student podcast that gives parents an idea of what's running through our students minds and how they are experiencing school. Allowing parents to access our podcasts makes it possible for them to listen while on the move. The response to the podcasts has been positive because families can listen together or individually and whenever they have the time.

The parents who cannot be reached by any of those avenues get home visits from me. Sometimes I walk students home, ride the bus, or just show up at their front doors when I feel we need to connect. One of our families who had not been to school in three days once got a big surprise when I rang their doorbell. I was welcomed into their home, and it was there that I learned their story. A relationship was formed, and this parent became an engaged member of our community. My visit showed them I cared and that I missed them when they weren't there.

Before I started at my current school, its story was being told by the people who made the most noise. Parent issues were being handled, but those issues were what everyone was talking about. Now we focus on sharing all the great things that are happening in our building daily. Changing the narrative has allowed our teachers the freedom to fail. Creating a positive parent community and story has shown parents that when our teachers and admin make mistakes, it will be okay. Not every parent will always be happy, and not every teacher will always be happy, but if we focus on what we're doing right, the negative will be outweighed by all the positive.

Be the One who engages your parent community and works with them to support students, making everyone more successful.

THINGS TO CONSIDER AND TWEET ━━━━━━━━━━━━━━━━

1. How do you engage your parent community?
2. How do you include them in their children's learning?
3. What has been the best thing about including families in your school?

━━━━━━━━━━━━━━━━━━━━━━━ #BETHEONE

WELCOME THEM
WITH OPEN ARMS.
#BETHEONE

13

BE THE ONE WHO DOES THE RIGHT THING

got married when I was twenty years old. Even as a little boy, I couldn't wait to be married and start a family. As soon as I got engaged, I knew I needed a job that would allow me to earn an honest living and provide for my soon-to-be family. I landed a position at a local bank, and I was excited to wear a suit! Coming from lifeguarding and coaching, this attire was a major shift in wardrobe. As soon as I started as a personal banker, I turned on my sales charm. As a personal banker, I was required to get a number of new accounts signed up. There was pressure to perform.

One practice I saw happening quite frequently was bankers adding accounts and reordering cards for people who didn't need them, but it made their numbers better. This became the norm, and we were being asked to cold-call people and sign them up for credit lines they didn't need. It was our job to convince them they couldn't live without it. I had to draw the line and take a stand. My moral compass said this was something that shouldn't be happening. I refused to lie to people about their accounts and capitalize on their vulnerability.

Moral and/or ethical dilemmas occur in every line of work. In education we have tons of gut decisions that sometimes we ignore. Testing, education practices, and the way we treat people sometimes go against what we believe to be what is best.

High school administrators are not always the most popular people. In this role, you're part safety supervisor, discipline officer, and detective. You wear multiple hats, and they rarely make you the campus favorite. When I had this job, I would walk the hallways and visit classrooms each day. When I got a tip about drugs, fights, academic dishonesty or anything else, I would follow up, making sure the truth was exposed, and correct the situation. It wasn't always easy, but I knew I needed to do the right thing far more than I needed to be liked.

One night while out with my wife, I saw a former student who happened to be a food runner at the restaurant where we were having dinner. At first, I ducked my head because I knew he and I'd had a rocky past. We'd had many conversations about drugs, academics, and how to get his life on track. He'd been suspended at the end of his sophomore year, and I had suggested he transfer to another local high school to make a fresh start for his junior year. Just as I finished telling my wife this story, he brought our salads to our table. "Hey, Mr. Sheehy," he said, recognizing me right away. We started talking, and he explained how appreciative he was that I'd held him accountable for his behavior back then. He had graduated high school and was working to earn a degree in aerospace engineering. It felt good to catch up with someone who had strongly disliked me for doing the right thing and see he was finally figuring it all out.

We must listen to our moral compass and Be the One who does the right thing.

THINGS TO CONSIDER AND TWEET ━━━━━━━━━━━━━━━

1. Have you faced a situation where doing the right thing was a difficult choice?
2. How do you change perceptions around doing the right thing?

━━━━━━━━━━━━━━━ #BETHEONE

DON'T LIMIT

LEARNING

#BETHEONE

14

BE THE ONE WHO PUTS A SMILE ON SOMEONE'S FACE

Smiling can make all the difference in the world. To some, that might sound trite, but I know without a doubt that it's true.

Berenice was a sophomore at the high school where I worked. She would always get to school early and stay extremely late. Her parents worked long hours, and she never wanted to be at home by herself, so she would hang out in the hallways. Those hallways were indoors, providing kids with a sense of safety, day or night.

On my morning walks to say good morning to students and teachers, I always noticed Berenice sitting or standing with her friends. Sometimes she would be talking, and other times she would be quiet, simply listening. The school year progressed and sometime in January, I realized Berenice was not in that group anymore. She had vanished. As I stopped to talk and greet her friends, I asked about Berenice. One of her friends said that her home life was horrible, and she had run away to Mexico. Of course, I didn't stop there but rather followed the proper steps and tapped into different resources to make sure she was checked in on. She was gone.

The first night she was gone, I sat there with a heavy heart. I thought about what else I could have done. Two weeks went by, and one of our school counselors came to find me. Berenice was back. She had realized she had no one in Mexico and thought things could be better where she knew people. She returned to school and met with the counselor. To this day, I still get choked up thinking about it. She told the counselor one of the main reasons she returned was because people at school smiled at her. She knew those people loved her and wanted the best for her.

Remember Berenice's story the next time you're rushing through your school's hallways. Try slowing down and smiling at students and teachers who cross your path. You never know—for some of those people, your smile could be the high point of the day.

THINGS TO CONSIDER AND TWEET

1. How do you put smiles on people's faces?
2. What does it take to put a smile on your face?
3. What are your top three strategies for getting people to smile?

#BETHEONE

CREATIVITY

HOW DO
YOU ENGAGE
{ YOUR }
PARENT
COMMUNITY?
#BETHEONE

15

BE THE ONE WHO CREATES MOMENTS FOR KIDS

Students had just finished reading the book *Wonder* in their classroom. They were studying empathy, and they wanted more than just having a conversation within the classroom. They wanted to start reading about empathy to other classes in the elementary school. They began to read the book *We Are All Wonders*. At the end of every reading session with the classes, the students led a discussion on what it meant to look and be different and how those people should be treated. This class of students took what they learned in their class and shared it with the school. As the principal, I was receiving messages from parents about the conversations that were being held at the dinner table. Of course, nothing made me happier than to hear these stories.

I reflected a lot on what was going on with these students. I thought of what I could do to reinforce the concepts and create a memory about which they would tell their grandchildren. I started by calling down to the local theater. I wanted to see if I could schedule a field trip to see the movie that had just been released based on the book they had recently read. After cutting through the red tape, the field trip was happening. Once students arrived at the theater, they were greeted with movie snacks and ushered into their private theater. Students were able to sit wherever they wanted and with their friends.

As I took my seat, I looked around the theater and looked into the eyes of the students. They were thrilled, and I knew the intentional work to get this organized was worth it. This was a memory about which they would be telling their grandchildren.

Looking through the eyes of kids, we as educators hold a great deal of power. Students love when they are encouraged, cheered on, loved, and recognized—especially by an educator in their lives.

As an elementary school student, I would walk around campus hoping to be recognized by someone for something I had to offer. My older brother was always being acknowledged for his reading skills or for following directions, while I was a rambunctious kid who loved being physical and social. As you can imagine, this caused some disruptions in the classroom. It is our duty as educators to recognize our kids for the amazing things they do.

Our childhood and school experiences ultimately shaped who we are today. Knowing how important encouragement from adults can be, I look for opportunities to encourage students in any way possible. Take the opportunity to get outside of the classroom and meet your students where they are. Whether it is fifth-grade camp, a soccer game, or running into them at the grocery store, encourage and create a memory.

Be the One who creates moments for everyone that create lifetime memories.

THINGS TO CONSIDER AND TWEET

1. How have you been a moment maker?
2. What will your students be telling their grandchildren about you?
3. What is one moment you have created?

#BETHEONE

16

BE THE ONE WHO OPENS STUDENTS' EYES

I grew up in Southern California and went to the beach every week during the summer. When we were not basking in the sun or splashing in the water, I was participating in some kind of outdoor activity. Whether playing an organized sport, building forts in the backyard, or camping with my family, I wanted to be—or was sometimes forced to be—outside.

Each summer we would pack our minivan and head to Yosemite National Park—my family's happy place. We would set up tents, hike, swim, bike, and enjoy all the park had to offer. Those trips showed me what the world was about and taught me to appreciate the outdoors and its beauty.

I often recall those experiences when I talk to students about attending our fifth-grade outdoor education camp and find out it will be the first time for some of them to ever get out of town or go on a hike. Being an avid hiker with my own kids, I am always surprised to hear that most families don't do this. Thanks to my families' annual trips to Yosemite, I know firsthand what those children are missing. We need to open our students' eyes to things they are not exposed to in their homes and communities.

Unfortunately, not every child is lucky enough to come from a family like mine and like many of yours. Families don't often camp, hike, bike, or even go outside together. Our high schools are being filled with students who don't understand the environment and how to utilize our natural resources to live a long and healthy life filled with many outdoor activities.

I am giving you the green light to tear down your classroom walls and open up your students' eyes to the wonderful world in which we live. Taking the walls down in your classroom and giving the students the opportunity to learn in a natural setting allows for conversations that will have an impact on their lives.

Whether it is technology or outdoor education, it is an educator's duty to give students new experiences that can change their lives forever. I challenge you to take your passion and share it with your students. Not only does it create a stronger teacher-student connection, it can teach kids to be more willing to try new things.

THINGS TO CONSIDER AND TWEET

1. What experience opened your eyes to education?
2. When was the last time you tried something new? How did it make you feel?
3. How can you give your students new experiences inside and outside of the classroom?

#BETHEONE

17

BE THE ONE WHO KNOCKS ON THE DOOR

Why wasn't that student in school today? What's going on with his family?

These are questions schools all over the world ask. Students vanish from our classrooms, and no one really knows what has happened. As a principal, I have students who move in and out of our attendance zone throughout the school year. One October, I got a call from the district office asking me to assist a new family to the area, and they wanted me to get them in contact with services that were available. All I knew was that they were a homeless family living in a friend's house in a pretty nice neighborhood. I greeted the family like any other family and welcomed them to our school.

Two weeks went by, and the kids were never on time, not even once. The mother used every excuse in the book—no gas, no electricity, slept late, kids were sick. I explained to her I wanted the best for the kids and would do anything I could to help. I reached out to a local college to see what types of services it could offer, and it was able to provide the family with gift cards to a local restaurant.

Another two weeks went by, then we didn't see the kids for five days. No call, no email, and no answer when we called. Where were they? What was going on? What had happened?

Doing what educators do when they are worried, I hopped into my car and headed to their house. Rounding the corner onto their street, I was surprised to see how nice the neighborhood was and how much pride of homeownership was displayed by all the surrounding houses. I found the house and got out, noticing their house was the most run down on the street, but still nice. I rang the doorbell and waited. Nothing happened—no noise, no movement. I rang the doorbell again. This time I saw shadows moving around behind the front window. I rang the doorbell a third time, and suddenly an older girl, high school age, answered the door, half asleep and in her pajamas. Rubbing her eyes, she did a double-take, yelling up the stairs, "Mom, the principal from the kids' school is here!" Mom yelled back, "Don't play; there is no way the principal is here." Soon Mom realized I was indeed standing at her front door.

She threw a blanket around herself and invited me in. As I entered the large home, I noticed there was no furniture. We started talking, and she explained they had no electricity and little food. Five of them shared a queen mattress, and to top it off, they all had lice. Wanting to help, I offered to go get lice shampoo, some furniture, and other donations. She refused any of the help and promised to have the kids back at school the next week. After about thirty minutes, I left the house and returned to campus, but I couldn't forget what I had seen.

The next week the kids were back at school, but Mom was nowhere to be found. It was an hour past pick up time, and she hadn't arrived. After quite some time, she called the school to say she had run out of gas and was walking, but she had no shoes on. When she got to the school, rather than lecturing her about being late, we showered her with love and generosity, resolving to start a donation drive for their family. Mom and kids began to weep. Moving from homeless shelters into a home was a scary process for them, but they were happy and grateful to be part of a caring community.

The kids are still late most days, but when they arrive, we shower them with love. We walk with them each day to breakfast and make sure they have what they need. Schools are families, and families wrap support around each other when needed. This relationship solidified when I knocked on their door, and the family realized we were invested in their welfare.

THINGS TO CONSIDER AND TWEET

1. Have you ever conducted a home visit? How was it received?
2. What are some of your reservations about visiting a student's home?
3. What was something good that happened because you knocked on a student's front door?

#BETHEONE

BREATHE AND GET OUTSIDE.
#BETHEONE

18

BE THE ONE WHO KEEPS KIDS MOVING

It was cold and rainy, but when you looked out into the field, there were seventy-five kids that didn't even notice the weather. Kids were smiling and having fun while getting muddy from the weather.

We had organized a flag football league in which students would stay late to play. Every week our group would get bigger and bigger. It was run in a tournament style; everyone was invited to participate, and everyone played. I bounced around and played quarterback from time to time. Kids loved it and would run home to tell their friends and families about it. The games went from being only after school to being part of our recesses and free time. The activity spread like wildfire, and I constantly had kids joining in. The idea of getting kids excited about moving had worked.

As I reflected about the flag football experience, it made me think about when I was in high school. Our school mascot was the Jaguars, and we ended every year in PE by participating in an activity called Jag Wars. It was a series of competitions that mixed students from all grade levels together on teams. The events lasted weeks and culminated with the winning team being awarded T-shirts at the end of the year.

I can remember looking around on those days, watching the competition and being surprised that some of the kids who were the highest performing were the kids who normally did not do anything in PE activities. But here we were in an environment where kids were having fun, and there was a sense of competition. Kids wanted to perform, and they wanted to be active.

I bring these stories up because they have impact. Too many of our children are sitting there not doing anything physical. We are losing the physicality we once had. It is our job as educators to keep our students moving and keep them healthy.

Be the One who challenges your students to be healthy and take the journey with them.

THINGS TO CONSIDER AND TWEET

1. How do you get kids excited about moving?
2. How do you model a healthy lifestyle for your students?

#BETHEONE

19

BE THE ONE WHO TELLS YOUR SCHOOL'S STORY

Every morning as I get ready for work and my kids get ready for school, there are two questions I ask. I ask these questions with one purpose. I want to make sure my kids are excited about school and learning.

What are you looking forward to today?

Are you doing anything fun at school today?

When the kids come home from school, I also check in and ask about their day. In our house, we typically do a roundtable at dinner to find out about everyone's day. These three questions lead the conversation:

What happened at school today?

What did you learn?

Who made an impact on you today?

Too often, negative reports are coming out about teachers, schools, and classrooms. It is our job as educators to shine a light on all the positive. That means we must tell our schools' stories. We must tell our communities—parents, businesses, and churches—how we are serving students, dealing with challenges, and celebrating our triumphs.

In my experience, however, many educators are a little scared to open up and tell their stories. We're afraid of being too honest, falling short of others' expectations, or having to share our failures.

But what are we really afraid of? Our job is not easy, yet so many of us pour everything we've got into teaching children day in and day out. I believe we're all pretty awesome, and we should be shouting about what's happening in our classrooms.

Consider these two questions: How do you connect with your families? How do you tell your classroom story? After I hear your answers to those questions, I can tell you about the climate and culture of your classroom.

Through the years, I have found that effectively telling a school's story hinges on making solid connections with the surrounding community. Here are some of my favorite tools that make the task just a bit easier:

1. BLOGS.

Blogging allows students and teachers a voice. It allows you to share your story with the world and allows students to develop as writers.

2. YOUTUBE.

With this platform you can capture on video all the amazing things happening in your school. Any time we have a special event on campus, we shoot some quick video on our GoPro and create a one- to two-minute video. Then we upload it onto my YouTube channel and share it via social media. By the time parents arrive for pickup, they have had the opportunity to see something of their children's day. YouTube also tracks how many people have watched your video and allows comments by subscribers.

3. PODCASTS.

Like blogging, podcasting gives you a voice, and it literally allows listeners to hear you. The first podcast I ever had was with a struggling student. He had been sent to my office with a referral, and I was running out of ideas to encourage him to improve his behavior choices. I told him I needed his help. We went over the idea of the podcast and began an interview. He was over the moon! It gave him an opportunity to connect with his family in a different way, and it was exactly what he needed.

4. TWITTER.

Twitter gives fellow educators and parents a window into your classroom and school. Educators can share awesome ideas through pictures on Twitter. I was at a meeting where I happened to run into the superintendent. She commented about how she loved that I have a 3-D printer in my office. She hasn't been in my office to see it, but she is seeing the interesting things we are doing with it on Twitter. It's a powerful place for connections.

5. WEBSITES.

School websites are the faces of your schools and should be treated that way! Too often websites are extremely outdated and filled with old content. Take the time to create teacher pages and maintain. Send out links to pages frequently, and make sure parents revert back to the website if they have questions.

6. NEWSLETTERS.

Do you send out a newsletter to parents? At some school sites, newsletters are a waste of time, while at others they are a necessity. If you use a newsletter that can run analytics, you can tell if you are being effective at getting the message out.

7. INSTAGRAM.

Instagram is another useful tool that allows you to showcase activities at your school and in your classroom. Many parents who are not on Twitter are on Instagram.

8. VOXER.

Voxer is an app that allows you to send voice and text messages to people all over the world without having their phone numbers. You can create groups on Voxer and have individual conversations as well. I currently belong to many different personal learning network (PLN) groups, and we meet via Voxer. At any point, I can pose a question on Voxer and get many different responses without having to be on my phone. I can listen to those messages as I walk between classrooms. I give my Voxer handle to parents, staff, and colleagues.

9. GREEN SCREEN APPLICATIONS.

This Green Screen application allows you to create high-quality videos with ease. When I arrived at my school, announcements were done via the loud speaker, interrupting classroom time and making it hard for students to hear. We switched to video newsletters that could be played when convenient for the teacher. We also have students record themselves on Green Screen giving reports with a pertinent green-screen background. My son recorded his report on Thomas Jefferson with a background of how Jefferson really looked.

No educator should ever miss an opportunity to say something good about their school. Every school has their own troubles, but there is always something amazing that happens at that school as well. Focus in on the good, and spread it like wildfire around your community. When we focus on the good, people expect the good—and it raises the bar for everyone.

Be the One who never passes up the opportunity to say something positive about your school.

THINGS TO CONSIDER AND TWEET

1. Who tells your school's story?
2. What are some of the obstacles you have encountered in telling your story?
3. How has taking control of telling your story shifted your school's climate?

#BETHEONE

LIFE IS AMAZING.
GO EXPERIENCE IT.
#BETHEONE

20

BE THE ONE WHO GETS OUTSIDE

It was 6:00 a.m.; three friends hopped into the car, and we headed to San Francisco. There is always traffic at that time of day, and we needed to make it to the school by 7:30 am. Arriving at the school early enough to see the arrival of students forever changed who I am as an educator. Every teacher was lined up out in front, and every child was greeted with a hug and an "I love you." It was something I had never seen before. The day was filled with moments of realization and self-discovery. As we talked, we learned of different ways to do things and simply walked away knowing that being an educator was an amazing opportunity and blessing.

This trip to visit another school came from an assignment in my credential program. We spent many hours visiting different schools and learning from a variety of educational leaders. To this day, I enjoy visiting different schools and talking with educators. We can learn so much by seeing and talking with others.

Talking with educators from all over the world has made me even more passionate about discussing how we focus on the word OUTSIDE. We can change instruction and make educators happier while becoming more effective.

1. Get up and get OUTSIDE of your office/classroom every day. Get into other classrooms and interact with different kids and teachers. For great things to occur, we must get

out of our bubbles and sometimes be uncomfortable. Build a reputation for being someone who is out and about, always looking to learn.

2. Don't be afraid of going OUTSIDE the norm. Each day we are faced with issues that require creative solutions if children are to be served well. That means we must summon the courage to try new things—even when others don't—to meet challenges as they arise.

3. Seek inspiration from new places. Sometimes you need an OUTSIDE perspective. It's healthy and fun to borrow ideas from professionals in other schools, neighboring school districts, TV shows, or even family vacations. Keep an open mind, and be ready to learn.

4. Get OUTSIDE and spend time together. It's my job as a parent to teach my kids to appreciate and respect nature. The best way to do that is by spending time with them outside—even if it's just for a few hours each weekend.

I challenge you to get OUTSIDE the office and classroom, to think outside the norm, learn from outside your school, spend time outside with those you love, and leave your personal issues outside school.

THINGS TO CONSIDER AND TWEET ━━━━━━━━━━━━

1. How do you take your classroom outside?
2. How do you think outside the norm?
3. How do you instill a love of the outdoors in your students?

━━━━━━━━━━━━━━━━━━━━ #BETHEONE

EMPOWERMENT

BRING ENERGY EVERYDAY.

#BETHEONE

21

BE THE ONE WHO BELIEVES IN KIDS

I didn't talk to my parents much about going to college until my junior year of high school. I absolutely loved high school, largely for the social aspect and the sports. Academics were tough, and I was always trying to live up to my parents' expectations. I was trying to live up to the standards my older brother had set. He was a 4.0 student who never seemed to get into trouble.

My dad would always remind me that I needed to take my studies more seriously. Both my mom and dad had high expectations of me balancing school and sports, and I was not allowed any extra-curricular activities unless my grades were good.

When the conversation with my parents turned to talking about college, dad said, "Ryan, college is not for everyone, and I don't think school is for you." I was taken aback and didn't know what to think. I knew he always thought that I didn't take school seriously, and he figured I shouldn't waste the money on tuition. There I sat, deflated by my dad's opinion, but I was still a motivated and determined individual. Since that conversation, his words have played over and over in my head. I often think about his reason for saying that to me. Was it to save money? Was he trying to motivate me? Did he really not think I was college material?

I knew I wanted more education, although I was unclear on what kind of degree I would pursue. Luckily I had others in my life who helped steer me in the right direction. We all need a cheerleader, someone in our corner. Telling a child, "I believe in you," is powerful praise.

As educators, we have so much power to influence our students. They walk into our schools each day trusting they are going somewhere safe where learning takes place. In the midst of that learning, we must build up our students' confidence instead of tearing it down. When counseling students on life and how certain behaviors can impact their futures, I always tell them I believe in them. It's true; I do.

Not all kids have parents at home who believe in them. The least we can do is believe in our students and help them know they can accomplish whatever they set their minds to. It is not always easy and there will be many bumps along the way, but a little support is exactly what some students need to succeed.

Choose your words wisely. If we are not careful, some statements can be misconstrued, leaving students to guess at your meaning. Be clear, be precise, and be their cheerleader.

THINGS TO CONSIDER AND TWEET

1. Who believes in you?
2. How do you show your students you believe in them? How do they know that you believe in them?
3. How can educators encourage students who have trouble believing in themselves?

#BETHEONE

22

Be the One Who Shows Respect, Kindness, and Love

It was a beautiful Friday afternoon, and I had just enjoyed a busy morning of visiting classrooms. By lunchtime I had bounced across campus from the playground to the cafeteria and back to the front office. When lunch ended, a group of students who were all riled up about something a classmate had done came charging into the office. Sixty seconds later, another wave of students joined them. With the waiting area filled to capacity, my attendance secretary gave me a look that said, "What just happened?"

The answer was simple—it was springtime. We had yet to have spring break, and the students—and probably a few teachers—were feeling the strain. They were ready for some time off, feeling stressed, and it was showing up in their behaviors.

At this point in the school year, it's often a daily occurrence to see a student, parent, or teacher crying. It happens every year without fail because stress is ever-present in our lives. But it's during these times of stress that we need to remember our purpose. Why are we here? Why are we in education? What are our goals? What can we do to move our students forward? How can we improve our students' learning experience?

When those questions run through my head, I am reinvigorated, and I want you to know. . .

- It is okay to be tired.
- It is okay to be frustrated.
- It is okay to feel stressed.
- It is okay to cry.

I also want you to know it is not okay to take frustrations out on parents, co-workers, supervisors, and most importantly, kids. It is our job to show students how to be resilient even when life is not easy, even when we have bad days. It is up to us to treat each other with respect, with kindness, and with love.

I will be the first to admit that I get weary. My patience has been tested over the years. Having said that, I wake up each morning resolving to be the best I can for my students and my staff. I am here to support them inside and outside of the classroom. We must check our baggage at the door and be all in when it comes to our students.

We must Be the One to show respect, kindness, and love.

THINGS TO CONSIDER AND TWEET ━━━━━━━━━━━━━━━━━

1. How do you model respect, kindness, and love?
2. What is one thing that helps you check your personal baggage at the door each day and be fully present for kids?

━━━━━━━━━━━━━━━━━━━━━━━━━━━ #BETHEONE

23

BE THE ONE WHO IS MAGICAL

After sitting through meeting after meeting, hearing about broken families, I started pondering a vacation for my own family. It occurred to me that one thing all families occasionally need to do is to slow down and make time for one another. Sitting there listening to stories about hurting families, I decided I needed to block out some time to spend with my family.

Compelled to act, I booked my family on a Disney Cruise. Growing up in Southern California, I had been to Disneyland several times but had only dreamed about taking a Disney Cruise. The experience was exceptional in so many ways. My family get some much-needed time together, and we were treated to Disney's world-class customer service. From the moment we boarded our ship in Miami, I noticed countless best practices I knew I wanted to replicate at my school. Here are a few of my favorites:

1. AN EXCITING WELCOME

As we entered the ship for the first time, the speakers proclaimed, "Disney's Magic welcomes the Sheehy Family!" That was followed by cheering from the crew members. Who wouldn't be excited to come to a place that cheers for you and is excited to see you?

In your schools, you get the opportunity to greet students and families every day. How do you show them your excitement? This is an area that is extremely important and needs to be done with intention.

2. EXCEPTIONAL CUSTOMER SERVICE

Disney is known for its customer service, and it did not lack on our ship. The wait staff and crew were constantly helping us with a smile and seemed to genuinely want us to enjoy our experience.

In our schools, we can be like that wait staff. All our employees—administrators, teachers, clerical staff, cafeteria workers—can provide exceptional customer service to our students and parents each day. Showing them we care has many benefits that will help students in the classroom. Every school employee needs to be trained to exemplify that high level of customer service.

3. OPPORTUNITIES FOR FUN

Around every corner, my kids found another fun opportunity. Whether we were watching movies, playing shuffleboard, shooting hoops, swimming, or flying down water slides, there was always one more activity on the horizon. There were so many options that everyone stayed busy, and no one got bored.

I believe we can do the same within our schools. We just need to channel some creativity into the classroom and fill our schedules with fun and proven activities students enjoy. Doing this keeps staff and students fully engaged and excited about learning new skills. It also helps keep educators from growing a little stale in their teaching practices.

4. EXCELLENT COMMUNICATION

Each night upon returning to our room from dinner, there was a communication flyer from the team at Disney. The paper would have all pertinent information and the details of the events planned for the next day. In addition to that hard copy, Disney also had an app that provided the same information.

At schools, communication is critical. We must communicate not only with our students and teachers but their families and the overall community. We must make sure our events are published and advertised so everyone in our community is able to plan and join in the fun. That means meeting our families where they are, communicating through phone, email, old-school print flyers, and word of mouth.

5. TEAMWORK

On our Disney cruise, it was clear every employee had a specific job. Seeing it in action, I found it astounding how well they adapted when a curveball got thrown. The employees had no problem stopping what they were doing to help out the others. Our waitress told us they work hard to function as a team, because for all of their guests to have an amazing time, all crew members must pull together.

In our schools, we all have individual jobs to do, but none of us can be successful without each other. We must remember to not only do the best we can but to also take time to help each other out.

These lessons from our Disney vacation can easily be applied in personal and professional settings. Take time to enjoy your family, recharge your batteries, and be the best for those who look up to you.

THINGS TO CONSIDER AND TWEET ━━━━━━━━━━━━━━

1. What magical experiences have you created for kids?
2. What could you add to your classroom or school to make it magical?
3. How do you encourage kids to be magical?

━━━━━━━━━━━━━━━━━━━━━━━ #BETHEONE

BE THE ONE WHO INSPIRES.
#BETHEONE

24

BE THE ONE WHO CONNECTS WITH KIDS

When things get busy at different times of the year, educators retreat to their offices and classrooms to get work done. I admit that closing my office door on all the chaos sounds appealing. Simply having time to plan and deal with the plant management components of running a school has a nice sound to it; however, we must fight the urge!

When you find yourself wanting to close your door, it's time to ask yourself, *How have I connected with kids today?* Due to parent meetings, Individualized Educational Plans (IEPs), and other office tasks, educators get bogged down and are not outside connecting with students as much as they should or would like. The good news? It's possible to reverse that trend. It just takes a little conscious effort to walk away from the paperwork for a few minutes each day and spend time with kids.

One day I made that effort and went on the swings with some of our students. We laughed, we talked, and they reminded me why I was there. Relationships matter! Spending time with kids inside or outside of the classroom can change their lives and yours.

Eleven years ago, when I was teaching fourth- and fifth-grade physical education at multiple elementary schools, I connected with a family, and an awesome relationship was formed. Eddie was a fourth grader who was being pulled into a life of gangs. He was looking for that one person who believed in him and wanted something different from him and for him. He came from a strong home with a wonderful mom and dad, but he just wanted to be cool like one of the neighborhood kids.

I was at Eddie's school every Tuesday. Whenever my PE team would go out on the blacktop, he would run over to fill me in on his struggles and victories of the week. We would talk at recess while jumping rope. We connected in such a way that he knew I believed in him and would be there if he needed it.

At the end of his fifth-grade year, he told me how much he loved soccer but said he didn't have a ball of his own. I decided I wanted to send him off to middle school with a new soccer ball. He was so excited when I gave it to him—the first time anyone ever asked for my autograph!

My wife and I still run into Eddie and his family occasionally at the grocery store. He has graduated from high school and is in college now. We always talk about the importance of the relationships he built with teachers throughout school.

My relationship with Eddie started with one simple conversation about his life. Take some time—even when you're tempted to hole up in your office—and show kids you care.

THINGS TO CONSIDER AND TWEET

1. How do you connect with your students?
2. What's it like, seeing your students, years later? What do they say?
3. What has been the best way to connect with your students?

#BETHEONE

25

BE THE ONE WHO
STAYS POSITIVE

When I interviewed for my first teaching position, I didn't realize the job started almost immediately; in fact, I had to report to school only two days after my degree posted. I was twenty-one years old and not sure what to expect. I was hired to be a physical education teacher at six different elementary schools with varying population, rotating daily to different schools. My classes were huge, anywhere from 90 to 120 students, but I did have the assistance of two instructional aides, who did little to hide their surprise when we met that first morning. "You are too young to be a teacher!" one of them said as I walked into the room. "I could be your mom!" said the other. Laughing awkwardly, I rolled with it. It was fifteen minutes before our first class would arrive, so we walked to the blacktop to set up. Rounding the corner, we found the ball wall had been tagged with several derogatory words. Perfect. I remember stopping and thinking, *What have I gotten myself into?*

I was clearly nervous, unsure, and psyching myself out. I took a few deep breaths, determined to stay positive. The principal was running around, frantically trying to get things cleaned up. I offered my assistance and showed I was more than a fresh-faced kid; I was a flexible professional who was willing to be part of the solution. When I think back to that first day, I believe that positive attitude started my education career on the right foot.

Few things in life—work, relationships, adventures—always go the way they should, but staying positive can make any situation a little better. Once I worked with an educator who brought that energy every day to the classroom and into the lives of her students. She was passionate, energetic, and enthusiastic about everything she did. I would watch the interactions that she would have with her students' parents, and you could feel the energy coming through, but it wasn't necessarily positive energy.

That is where the distinction needs to be made. We must bring the energy each day, but it needs to be positive. This individual teacher was energetic when it came to making students feel good about themselves and feeling self-pride. She would hand out three raffle tickets, and as the week went on, students would lose them if their behavior was not on point. At the end of the week, the students would put their remaining tickets into a raffle. This teacher thought it was amazing, and she was full of energy around it. When I asked her about flipping it and giving raffle tickets for amazing things, something happened to her thinking. She realized the positivity she thought she was bringing was, in fact, negative. Educators need to think carefully and consciously about bringing positive energy into the classroom each day.

At a recent principals meeting, a colleague shot me a look and asked, "Why are you so happy? I look on your social media, and you are always having fun." I looked at her, smiled, and agreed. I told her we all need positivity in our lives. And if you can't be positive, try to fake it—for the sake of your students, parents, and co-workers. Like so many other things, it's a choice we can make every day.

Staying positive changes the way we and our colleagues look at life; it also creates the right environment with our students. Be the One who remembers to stay positive even when times are tough.

THINGS TO CONSIDER AND TWEET

1. How do you stay positive?
2. What is your go-to strategy when you cannot shake a negative attitude?
3. How do you help your students stay positive?

#BETHEONE

FIX TARDINESS WITH ENGAGEMENT.

#BETHEONE

26

Be the One Who Inspires Kids

It does not matter who you are—everyone needs to be inspired. We all have days that are hard, days that are unbearable, days that take everything to survive. On those days, we need inspiration to make a difference.

When students leave our classrooms and schools, they should be able to walk away with some of these key life lessons they can put into practice:

1. KEEP A POSITIVE ATTITUDE.

Your attitude impacts everyone around you. If you choose to have a positive attitude, you might be able to change other people's attitudes, which can make life more pleasant for everyone.

2. SMILE AND LAUGH OFTEN.

Both spread positivity without saying anything.

3. BE YOURSELF.

There is only one you, so never try to be like someone else. Be confident in who you are. We care more about cultivating the person you are rather than helping you become someone you are not.

4. IT'S OKAY TO FAIL.

Success is great, but we learn the most when we make mistakes. Failure is part of learning, so keep a growth mindset. The more you continue to put yourself out there, the more you grow. Remember, FAIL means First Attempt In Learning. We must all fail in order to learn.

5. HAVE MENTAL TOUGHNESS.

This means you must work hard and never give up, even when life is challenging. Throughout your life, you will encounter many challenges, but you must determine to be tough and never give up.

6. NEVER STOP DREAMING.

Keep imagining your future. You are here for a reason, and you will make a difference in this world if you set goals for yourself. Think and dream about your future. Sit down and write goals on how you will achieve your dream.

7. BE HONEST.

Honesty is one of the most important traits someone can have. With honesty comes respect from others.

8. LIFE IS WHAT YOU MAKE OF IT.

Surround yourself with people who support you, push you, and challenge you to become better.

9. BE KIND.

Never forget how powerful your words are. Throughout your life, you will have opportunities to make the easy choice with your words, and you will have the choice to make hard decisions with your words. Choose to be kind, and use your power for good.

10. KNOW THAT I BELIEVE IN YOU.

I hope you always remember your time in my classroom. I care about you, and I want to see you be the best you.

Some educators put character development solely on parents and do not believe it is the school's responsibility, but educators spend more time with kids than most parents do. So shouldn't we be modeling the behavior that shows students how to be honest, kind, and compassionate?

Be the One who inspires, no matter the situation.

THINGS TO CONSIDER AND TWEET

1. What inspires you to be better?
2. What are three ways you inspire students daily to be better people?

#BETHEONE

RELATIONSHIPS MATTER.
#BETHEONE

27

BE THE ONE WHO TEACHES KIDS IT'S OKAY TO FAIL

When Robert was five, he wanted to play basketball. He was tall for his age, so there were many coaches who would talk to us about having him play for their team. Not that they had ever seen him play, but apparently at five, if you are tall, you have a huge advantage. He attended the practices leading up to the games and suddenly got discouraged. There was an adult telling them that if they weren't making it into the bucket, that was failing. The kids' faces were demoralized.

This aggravated me in so many ways. I decided to keep my cool and work with my son on the definition of *fail* and how the word shouldn't have such a negative connotation at five years old.

What does it mean to fail?

How do you explain failure to your students?

How do you help them deal with failure when it happens?

Starting every academic year talking with students about failure can be scary. It's a conversation that can be as powerful as it is overwhelming.

If you tell your students it's okay to fail because FAIL stands for First Attempt In Learning, you are setting the tone for a successful year.

Whenever we take a leap of learning and put ourselves in a position where it is possible to fail, we are vulnerable. This vulnerability is powerful, and it is what drives our learning. It is your job and educational responsibility to show your students it is okay to fail as long as they are willing to try something new.

I like the story about a basketball player who shot fifteen free throws and missed only two baskets. He was proud of himself. He strutted around the court and asked a friend how many shots he'd missed. His friend admitted he'd missed eight baskets. The first player grinned in triumph, but he sobered pretty quickly when his friend added that he'd actually taken a total of 100 shots.

It's not only okay to fail—you need to fail harder!

When our students leave our schools, they need to know it is okay to make mistakes. For that to happen, they will have to see us fail, dust ourselves off, and try again.

Reflect on your practices, and think of how you can model what it looks like to be a risk taker. Be the One who lets our students know it is okay to FAIL.

THINGS TO CONSIDER AND TWEET

1. How do you model risk taking for your students?
2. What do you do if one of your students takes a risk and does not succeed?
3. What has been your biggest failure, and what did it teach you?
4. If you take a risk, are you unleashing potential?

#BETHEONE

— 28 —

BE THE ONE WHO CREATES POSITIVE SCHOOL MEMORIES

Early one summer, while interviewing counselors for a position at my school, a candidate made the comment, "Kids don't remember what teachers taught them; they remember how teachers treated them." This quote has stuck with me and made me reflect on my own school experiences and what I remember about the teachers who have been in my life.

I admit I can't remember specific details about the lessons I had. I can, however, remember how teachers treated me, and I do remember the details of some of those interactions:

Kindergarten: She was so much fun. She rode trikes alongside us, and she always had a huge smile. I can remember her sitting alongside me while playing in the sandbox, digging side by side.

First Grade: She shared her passion of reading with us, and she had a unique sense of dental hygiene. Each day she would have us brush our teeth after lunch. It was her way of teaching us an important life skill. All the students in the class were treated like her grandchildren.

Second Grade: She took the time to get to know her students, and she helped me believe in myself. A few times when we were not in school, she invited students back onto campus for hang-out times. Small groups of kids would get to connect with her and build strong relationships.

Third Grade through Fifth Grade: My teacher was my mom, and it was a struggle to shift from mom to teacher and from son to student and back again, but we had many great adventures and learned a lot of different things. Being together so much caused the relationship to become strained, which hurt the education. Relationships are so crucial to see kids succeed. Even though the time strained our relationships, lots of great things happened too.

Sixth Grade and Seventh Grade: This teacher took a tough-love approach, and for any infraction would assign me writing the same sentence five hundred times. She demanded respect from her students but did not always take the time to earn it.

Eighth Grade: At the start of this particular year, our teacher took the time to build a team of students who wanted to learn together. This move created a classroom culture where students felt comfortable.

High School: I had many teachers who cared more about course content than they did about their students. Two teachers who cared more about their students were my photography teacher and my PE teacher. We spent time talking together, and they established lasting relationships with me. I was always willing to do pretty much anything they asked. They knew how to use relationships to build capacity in students to do different things.

It's no accident that these are the school memories that stand out for me. These teachers took time to get to know me, understand my interests and limitations, and encourage my efforts. That's what sticks with a child for years to come. I challenge you to reflect on your own primary and secondary education experiences and see what you remember. Be the One who creates positive school memories for your students.

THINGS TO CONSIDER AND TWEET ━━━━━━━━━━━━━━━

1. How do you establish relationships?
2. What do you think your students will remember about you?
3. What do you remember about your own teachers?

━━━━━━━━━━━━━━━━━━━ **#BETHEONE**

LOVE
{ TO READ. }
#BETHEONE

29

BE THE ONE WHO TEACHES BALANCE

What is balance? Is it something we are born with or is it something we are taught? Each day, countless high school students end up in a counselor's or principal's office because they struggle with balance.

Today's students are under so much pressure, and that pressure starts at an early age. Kids are trying to live up to so many expectations while also making sure they have a good college resume. For some, the planning starts as early as elementary school.

As a high school administrator, students would come to the office and want to just sit and talk about the pressure they were under. It wasn't high school drama—this student's struggle was real. This teenager was a student leader, an amazing athlete, and had a full load of AP classes and many friends. She also played club athletics to make sure she was noticed, studied "all night" to get good grades, and lost a lot of sleep making sure all her school events went off without a hitch. She had always dreamed of one day becoming a college athlete, and she had the brain and skills to make that dream come true. But all that excellence took a toll. Some days she would have it all together, and on other days she was overwhelmed and depended on our team to help her prioritize.

During our office talks, we would discuss how difficult it was to live a balanced life. We tried to help her understand it's not easy to be pulled in many different directions but manageable when you are clear about what you want out of life. We talked about her goals. Coming into her senior year, she needed balance in her life. She created a list of things that were important and things that she could live without. Using those lists as way to balance her life, she set up priorities so too many things were not happening at once.

It is some people's nature to want to do everything; however, it is not always practical or possible to squeeze everything into our lives. Constantly jamming things into our days will create individuals who are stressed, not happy, and extremely overscheduled. Teach balance, and demonstrate it in your life.

THINGS TO CONSIDER AND TWEET

1. What's the hardest part about finding balance?
2. How do you make time for everything you want to get done daily?
3. How do you teach balance to your students?

#BETHEONE

30

BE THE ONE WHO TURNS LIFE INTO A LESSON

Growing up in an extremely traditional family, I loved my parents unconditionally and always thought there was no one else out there who would treat me the same way. After meeting my wife's father, I was proven wrong. We created a friendship, a camaraderie, and a father-son relationship that rivaled many real father-son relationships. One night our world was turned upside down. At 12:30 a.m., our phone rang, and knowing that no one calls in the middle of the night with good news, I sat up and waited for my wife to answer. Within seconds, I heard screams of terror coming from the kitchen where she answered the call. My wife's father had passed away suddenly and unexpectedly.

He was a jack-of-all-trades, a man who had traveled, served our country, and was loved by many. At the time of his death, I went from being in full school mode to needing to completely remove myself from school and be with my family. It was a sad and difficult time, but you learn to keep moving through the grief. Here's some of what I learned from that experience:

1. BUILD RELATIONSHIPS.

We are constantly being pulled in different directions and don't always spend enough time building relationships. This is becoming more and more common in our digital age, where face-to-face communication is becoming less common. Take an interest in the people around you and be present to serve when you are needed. The journey is much sweeter when we take it together.

2. CHERISH YOUR TIME.

If there is something in life you want to do, do it! I am constantly creating lists of things I want to do, but I'm not always sure I will get the opportunity. Life is short, so when the chance comes, jump on it. Get active, stay healthy, and make sure you're around to do the things you want.

3. WORK WILL ALWAYS BE THERE.

When my father-in-law died, I had to put work on the back burner. I had to walk away, leave things undone, and trust someone else to step in. It was uncomfortable and frustrating, but my wife and kids needed me more. We all needed time to mourn and be together, and the reality was, there would always be more work to do. The break was a good one, and I was able to simply be present with my family and friends, offering and receiving the support we all needed.

In this life, we all get thrown curve balls, but we can survive them and learn from them. Build relationships, set your priorities, and be present for all that life has to offer. Don't be afraid to Be the One who shares lessons learned with colleagues and students. We all have so much to learn from each other and the life we live.

THINGS TO CONSIDER AND TWEET ━━━━━━━━━━━━

1. How do you take curve balls and turn them into life lessons?
2. How do you discuss life lessons with your students?
3. What is something in your life from which you have learned?

━━━━━━━━━━━━━━━━━━━━━━ #BETHEONE

31

BE THE ONE WHO SAYS IT'S OKAY TO CHANGE THE DREAM

When I was a young boy, I dreamed of being a cattle rancher and a professional baseball player. My brother and I would work our ranch together, and he would take over while I went away during baseball season. At the time, Nolan Ryan was my favorite player because he was a cowboy and baseball player. I thought he had it all figured out. That was my dream.

As time went by, my dream morphed into a lot of different things. I wanted to work in the financial district, be an entrepreneur, a father, and finally, an educator. My dreams continue to change, but that's okay—at least I'm still dreaming.

As a high school administrator, I had the opportunity to work with students who were preparing to go to college and chase their dreams. I met one of those students when she was just a sophomore. She was a water polo player with a 4.0 grade point average, the class president, and eventually, associate student body president. Her dream was to play water polo at the collegiate level. She had been playing club water polo for years and swimming since she was four years old. She would often come into my office and talk about her dreams and her lofty-but-attainable goals. Like many high-achieving kids, she had good days and bad. For the next two years, I helped her celebrate when things went well and helped her de-stress when life got crazy. I offered advice from my days as a coach and offered the counsel of an educator.

Senior year came, and she was right on target for a college scholarship and her dream of being a college athlete. Multiple schools were knocking at her door, and she and her family were excited about her future. As graduation approached, she admitted to herself and everyone else her dream had changed. For years, she had pushed herself to be able to play water polo in college, but she finally realized she wanted a more balanced life. She chose a school that wasn't top-tier and didn't have an NCAA water polo team— just a club program. Though she was afraid of what others might say and worried about disappointing loved ones, she was honest with herself and followed her gut. When she delivered her graduation speech, she encouraged her classmates to follow their dreams and not be afraid to adjust those dreams when interests change.

It is okay to change your dreams, and our students need to be reminded of it. It is not okay to stop dreaming. If we stop dreaming, it is like part of our soul has died. Be the One who encourages dreaming and lets them know it is okay to change the dream along the way.

THINGS TO CONSIDER AND TWEET

1. What dreams have you had that eventually changed into something different?
2. How do you let your students know it's okay to change their dreams?

#BETHEONE

32

BE THE ONE WHO IS REAL

Be Real. It seems so simple, but so often we come across people who are anything but real. Just watch TV, flip through a magazine, or scroll through Facebook. We live in a world where people tell you what you want to hear or what might get them what they want. The truth is not necessarily at the top of the list. I hear people all the time claiming they stand for something, but their actions say something completely different. Our words hold power until they don't match up with our actions, and then those words are just words. When we surround ourselves with people who are real, life is infinitely richer.

I once had an interview for a vice principal job at an elementary school, and at the end, I was asked to give a closing statement. I was well-versed in the closing statement, but on that day, I decided against my go-to response. I decided to be real. I told the panel it would be getting six people if I was the candidate hired because my wife and four children would become part of the school community. I told them I was a passionate educator, but I was a father and husband first and would not sacrifice my family for the job. As politely and professionally as possible, I added that if they wanted someone who would be at the school every night until eight o'clock, I was not their guy. I would be going home in the evening to see my family and would likely work from home after my kids were in bed.

Too often we keep quiet and don't challenge things that we are being told. Too often we sit in meetings and just go with it. We let the loud-voiced people in our lives run with their ideas and things they think are best. Stand up and be real. Let them know what you think and how you think things should be done.

There is no good reason to abandon your personal ideals to tell someone what they want to hear. Throughout my career, I have been honest about my family coming first, and I think it has helped far more than it has hurt. Every year I explain to parents they will not find me at school late at night because I will be at home with my family. My honesty, I believe, helps parents understand I am dedicated to my children, and I make decisions as both an educator and a dad. I don't always see eye-to-eye with parents, but I think they trust I am working in the best interests of their children.

We must resist the urge to tell our students and parents only what they want to hear. We must show our kids it's best to be genuine, to be themselves.

THINGS TO CONSIDER AND TWEET

1. Have you ever come across someone who was fake? How did you handle it?
2. How do you teach students to embrace who they are and stay true to themselves?

#BETHEONE

33

Be the One Who Creates Ownership

I was a second grader, and my older brother was in fifth grade. He was about to transition to the middle school located right next to the elementary school. My parents were concerned for his safety because he was the type of kid that would step between two kids fighting. My parents were so concerned, they decided to home-school us.

After three years of being homeschooled, I was able to get my parents to agree to send to me to a school. It was a private Catholic school that had a student population of twenty-three (K–12). The only issue with the school was that it was private, and tuition was higher than my parents could afford. My mom was determined to make this school happen for us. One of our family members offered to help pay the tuition, and my mom was able to work out a deal with the school for the rest.

Since the school was in their first year, it didn't have all the custodial positions filled or created. Every Saturday, my mom, brother, and I would go to the school early in the morning. We would spend about half of our day cleaning every room in the school. My parents would do whatever it took to make sure we got the education they wanted us to have.

No one knew what we did on Saturdays, but nevertheless, I felt a sense of embarrassment while cleaning the classroom where

I would sit during the week; however, this every week gave me a sense of ownership of the school. While in class, if I saw trash on the ground, I would hurry over and pick it up.

Fast forward many years to where I am today. We look for ways to create ownership in schools. Students, parents, and educators should have that same feeling of rushing over and picking up a piece of trash on the ground. This is our home, this is our house, and we want everyone to help out where needed.

There is no job too big or too small for any member of our school community. Help out, and build each other up.

THINGS TO CONSIDER AND TWEET ▬▬▬▬▬▬▬▬▬▬▬▬

1. How do you create ownership?
2. If all your students felt ownership of the school and would do whatever it took, what would be possible?

▬▬▬▬▬▬▬▬▬▬▬▬▬▬▬▬▬▬▬ #BETHEONE

34

BE THE ONE WHO BUILDS THEM UP

It was mid spring, and my classmates were excited! In a few weeks, we would be heading out to summer—and would return as seventh graders! My sixth-grade class consisted of six boys, and that was it. That's right, the entire sixth grade at my small private school was six kids. That one day in spring, the entire grade level was about to change. One morning our teacher informed us we would be having a visitor. There was a young girl who wanted to check out the classroom to see if it would be a good match for her as a seventh grader.

As the girl and her family toured the classroom, I remember looking across the room at my classmates and seeing things being done that shouldn't in a class of six. Some of my classmates made rude comments, and some paid zero attention to the teacher when all eyes were supposed to be on her.

As our classroom visitor left the room, the teacher turned to us with a face of mortification. It was a face of disappointment, dissatisfaction, and surprise all in one. We had let her down. She did her scolding routine and told us to think about it before we left for the day.

As we entered the room the next day, something was different; the temperature of the room was off. All six of us took our seats and were ready to start our day as the teacher walked in. She had the same face as the day before and began telling us all about it. She was upset, disappointed, and disgusted with our behavior from the day before. She started to tell us about what we would learn from this and how we would never act the same again. She said this was a learning opportunity, and she proceeded to explain how we would learn it.

All students were assigned to write "I will never be rude or disrespectful when a visitor enters our classroom." We were to spend however many recesses it would take to write this phrase 1,500 times. None of us were happy, but we knew we had to do it.

This experience has stuck with me for years. It had a direct effect on me and how I deal with students. Kids will make mistakes and challenge your thinking. It is situations like this that shape students' opinions and perceptions of school.

Middle school can be a tough time for all students. Bodies are changing, and students are trying to figure out who they are as individuals and what they want their identity to be. Be the One who helps fix mistakes. Let's build each other up.

THINGS TO CONSIDER AND TWEET ════════════════

1. How do you build students up in the classroom?
2. How do you handle students who don't respect each other?

═══════════════════════════════ #BETHEONE

CONTINUED LEARNING

MAKE SOMEONE SMILE TODAY.
#BETHEONE

35

BE THE ONE WHO LOVES THE JOB

L et's be honest. There comes a time every year where most people in education are counting down to the last day of school.
I am no different. By late spring, I am excited about spending more
time with family and simply having some time off. At the same
time, I am sad to see the year end. I love my students and colleagues
and the strides we make together throughout the year. From my
first year of teaching to where I am today, I have had an amazing
career. Just thinking about the journey puts a smile on my face. Of
course, they have not all been easy, but they have been pretty great.

Every day I have conversations with friends who have chosen
all kinds of career paths—finances, construction, farming, med-
icine, and even the oil business. Typically, after a few minutes of
talking about our jobs, they'll pause and add with a bit of amaze-
ment, "Ryan, you really have fun at work!" Yes, I do! I love my job.

My career took me to twelve schools as a teacher and two more
as a vice principal before I became an elementary school principal.
For the first four years teaching, I was a traveling physical education
teacher, teaching at six schools per week. The journey was not easy,
but it was extremely worth it. It has taken me to the point that I
love my job, and I have fun every day. I get to wake up each day and
spend time with teachers, parents, and students.

Do you have fun at work?

When you do, what makes that happen?

The days that I get to crawl on the ground with kindergartners, sit in bean bags with first graders, or just sit and hang with fifth graders are precious. I get to see what learning looks like through their eyes. This was not always the case. There were many difficult days when I found myself wondering if I had chosen the right career path. In time, I figured out I was in exactly the right place. I also learned the importance of choosing to have a positive attitude and mindset every single day. No matter how much someone loves their job, there will be tough days. When you pull into the parking lot, do your best to leave the negativity in the car, and walk into your school with a positive attitude.

Are you making a difference? I believe we all want to make a difference and work with purpose.

When I was a first-year principal—as if I wasn't busy enough—I accepted an offer to be an adjunct professor. The class I taught was a credential class for special education teachers, many of whom were already in the classroom. One day, as the class wrapped up, one of my students approached and thanked me for renewing her love of education and restoring her faith in the system. She caught me off guard. She continued to say she could see that I loved my job and wished more people shared that passion for kids. This is the reason we choose to be educators. We all have the power to unleash each other's potential to Be the One for Kids.

Love your job, and your passion shines through.

THINGS TO CONSIDER AND TWEET ━━━━━━━━

1. When things get tough, how do you relieve the pressure and have some fun?
2. How do you make a difference at your school? In your classroom?
3. How do you model loving your job so kids want to be educators?

━━━━━━━━━━━━ **#BETHEONE**

FOCUS ON WHAT'S IMPORTANT.

#BETHEONE

36

Be the One Who Prepares Kids for the Future

Five years ago, no one would have thought coding and 3-D printing would be a common practice in our classroom and across our schools. At our school, all our classrooms are coding using Sphero® robots and code.org. For our advanced coders, we have drones and 3-D printers. The reality is that most elementary school students don't have access to this kind of technology at home, and I feel it is our duty to introduce them to these tools because, by the time they are out of school, these industries are where the jobs will be.

We send these tools home with students so they can learn alongside their parents as a family, and the practice has proven to be very beneficial to our school community. This approach can apply to parents, teachers, administrators, and everyone who wants to be productive. We must resist the temptation to get stuck in the present and strive to keep our eyes open and looking to the future.

Every Friday, as the bell rings, students quickly line up outside the front office door. You expect on Friday afternoons for students to quickly go home and start their weekend. Not at our school. Students have the opportunity to keep their relevant learning all weekend long. Students line up to check out a Sphero for coding and other robotic-type activities. These devices are sent home with students, allowing them to show their families what they are doing and how it is relevant to today and the future.

Today's future looks different than tomorrow's future. We must continue to investigate and determine what is relevant. Kindergarten programs are focusing on what is happening fourteen years down the road and the skills needed to be successful then. All this is done while building the foundation for all education.

This concept seems to be easier in high school, where the future is literally at our student's fingertips. Look at how our schools are set up, and make sure we are preparing each for tomorrow.

As we go through the year and look at ways to redesign classrooms and curriculum, we need to always keep present and future industries in mind. So often we study how things were done in the past and forget to look to the future and the strides being made around us. Students need skills and knowledge that are relevant in today's world and can equip them for the world to come.

Schools must provide real-life examples for students to stay engaged and thrive in their environments. That means creating opportunities for students to pursue their joys and hobbies in the classroom. Coding is a skill we are using at our school to break down walls and forge new connections with students. It's allowing us to show kids how critical thinking skills are relevant, fun, and important for life. Students can see what industries need coders and how those skills can provide life-changing opportunities. Students are never too young to learn skills that will help them plan for their futures.

As you do this, be sure to allow students to talk to each other about these new interests and skills. It's pretty discouraging to walk into a classroom and be greeted with silence. Remember, Silent students = No collaboration. Some teachers might resist this idea, arguing that their students don't know how to work together. Those teachers are correct. It is our job to teach students how to collaborate and how to function as a team.

Be the One who stays up with the times and makes sure content is current and relevant.

THINGS TO CONSIDER AND TWEET

1. How do you make learning relevant?
2. How are you preparing students for the world of the future?
3. How can you foster more collaboration in your classroom?

#BETHEONE

WHAT'S YOUR POWER?

#BETHEONE

37

BE THE ONE WHO REFLECTS

As the academic year comes to a close, every teacher should take a moment and reflect on how the year went and what can be improved moving forward. Throughout this process, it is important to ask questions that will help you evaluate your effectiveness. Here are a few of my favorites:

1. HOW DO YOU STAY ORGANIZED?

As an educator, you will constantly have challenges to face. Without the ability to stay organized, you will struggle in assessments and classroom management. Being organized allows for quick transitions and less down time, which in return means fewer behavioral problems. Classrooms need to be focused and driven with purpose and relevance.

2. HOW FLEXIBLE ARE YOU?

It's a Friday morning, and one of your grade-level team members is sick. Although the teacher put in for a substitute, no one showed up. This is a common and consistent scenario across the country, but it doesn't have to ruin the day for you or your students. It just might take a few deep breaths, an open mind, and some creative thinking. Remember, the key is being flexible in all kinds of situations and giving your students your best.

3. HOW DO YOU STAY CREATIVE?

Being an educator means creating activities designed to master skills within a productive learning environment. At any given moment, opportunities can arise to capture new ideas for your classroom. You never know where your latest inspiration will come from—a TV show, your child's gymnastics class, or a stroll around the mall. Being able to take an idea and mold it into a fun and exciting activity your students will enjoy creates a buy-in from students and makes you an amazing educator.

4. WHAT MOTIVATES YOU?

Unfortunately, many parents I talk to describe their own school days with lots of negatives. Too often they describe educators who had given up and were not motivated to be at their best. Educators need to stay motivated and eager to learn and grow. A motivated educator takes opportunities to learn new things and strives to be a leader in the field. Educators who attend conferences/workshops tend to have students who experience a more positive school environment. Overall, motivated educators extend their education, look for opportunities for growth, seek out those who are successful and try to learn from them, and see what they can work into their programs.

5. HOW PATIENT ARE YOU?

Patience is a trait that needs to be exercised daily in school. As an educator, you are going to see a wide range of skill levels and abilities from students. The first time I ever taught first graders, I was not sure I would be able to survive them. They were more concerned about the butterflies than what was going on in class. With patience and classroom management, it is possible to hold the attention of younger students and bring great joy to your classroom.

6. HOW DO YOU COMMUNICATE WITH STAFF AND YOUR PEERS?

Being an effective communicator with other educators about your program is very important. Open communication will increase the credibility of your program and everything you do on a daily basis. If the school buys into your program, the rewards of this partnership transfer to the students. Showcase what you are doing in the classroom, and encourage others to ask about it. Creating open dialogue moves your school forward.

7. HOW DO YOU COMMUNICATE WITH PARENTS?

Creating a website and using a variety of social media platforms and other communication tools allow the school community to discover all the great things happening in your classroom and school. Asking school leaders for opportunities to share your program at parent-teacher association meetings is a great way for you to share with families what is going on in your class. It's also a great way for parents to become enthused about what their child is learning and experiencing in their educational journey. Overall, being an effective communicator with the school community can lead to fundraising, grants, and opportunities for growth in your classroom.

8. WHAT DO YOU DO TO BE A LEADER IN YOUR BUILDING?

You have the power to get students enthused about many different things in school. Students tend to gravitate toward teachers, looking for guidance on what is—and isn't—fun and exciting. What are you doing to get your student population enthused about learning? Nothing looks better for your program than helping lead the school in committees and instruction.

9. WHAT DO YOU DO FOR FUN?

Last but not least, have fun! If you are not having fun on the job, how are your students supposed to get excited about school? Why would they want to become educators? Your job is to get students so interested in the activities they're doing that they will turn into lifelong learners.

Self-evaluation must become a habit. It must be something that is used for growth, and we can never get to a place where we don't practice self-evaluation. It allows us time to reflect on what has worked and what hasn't. Most importantly, it helps us evaluate the direction in which we are going—as well as our goals and our visions for the coming year.

THINGS TO CONSIDER AND TWEET

1. How often do you self-reflect?
2. How do you encourage students and peers to reflect on their work and evaluate their own performance?
3. What have you learned about yourself through self-reflection?

#BETHEONE

38

BE THE ONE WHO
ASKS FOR FEEDBACK

ow am I doing? What do I need to do to improve? How can I
better serve my students?

These are questions that go through educators' minds on a consistent basis. We can and should evaluate our own work, but it's especially helpful, even necessary, to ask others for feedback. If you never ask for feedback on the job you are doing, you are only guided by your own perceptions and beliefs. When that happens, educators run the risk of becoming self-proclaimed experts or totally resistant to change.

As a high school vice principal who was relatively young compared to the teaching staff, I was assigned three departments to evaluate along with many other duties. One of the departments I supervised was the science department, which had struggled with teacher turnover in previous years. I met with one of the teachers who had been teaching longer than I had been alive, of which he reminded me frequently. We talked about his goals and the standards on which he wanted to focus in the upcoming year. I laid out my goals and the standards on which I wanted us to work. After we finalized the goals, we set up our formal observations, which would take place throughout the year. After each of those formal observations, we met to discuss his performance and areas for growth. The meetings were cordial and sparked great conversation. The feedback was purposeful, direct, and timely.

As the year wrapped up, I asked that teacher to write down his impression of the goals set up at the beginning of the process before we met for the formal evaluation. When we sat down for our meeting, everything changed. The dialogue focused on areas of growth and areas where more attention needed to be spent. The teacher had never before received constructive feedback. He had always heard, "You are doing fine." He told me I was too young to give him feedback and that students "received a gift" when he was assigned as their teacher.

The teacher had never asked for feedback, and the feedback he had received wasn't honest or effective. As a result of receiving no feedback, his teaching had grown stale. He had never been challenged, and he depended on his own views of how he thought he was doing.

We all must ask for feedback and remember that when we give feedback, it should be productive. Feedback is not an opportunity to tear someone down, but to help them grow. Here are three simple questions you can ask others when seeking feedback:

1. What's one thing I can do to help you become more successful?
2. What's one thing I should stop doing because it is not effective, or you don't like it?
3. What's one thing I should keep doing to be effective?

These are simple questions, but if used effectively, they can help you grow as an educator.

THINGS TO CONSIDER AND TWEET ━━━━━━━━━━━━━━━━━━

1. When is the last time you asked for feedback?
2. What have you learned about yourself by asking for feedback?
3. If you could change the way feedback is given, what would it look like?

━━━━━━━━━━━━━━━━━━━━━━━━ **#BETHEONE**

NO EXCUSES.

WE MUST

DO MORE.

#BETHEONE

39

BE THE ONE WHO PUTS YOURSELF OUT THERE

There I was, a college transfer to California State University-Hayward. My girlfriend (now my wife) was a swimmer and water polo player for the university. I attended all the sporting events and cheered on my friends and classmates, but I knew something was missing.

Before transferring, I had been a water polo player and member of the swim team at the community college I attended. My coach had lined up a couple of schools back east that were considering offering me a scholarship, but I was conflicted over whether I should chase my athletic dreams or move with my girlfriend to her school. I chose to follow my heart.

When I got there and saw all the fun things being offered, I realized I wanted to continue my own collegiate athletic career. The university didn't offer men's swimming or water polo due to Title IX constraints. By the end of my first year, I decided I needed to be part of a team. I had three options—basketball, baseball, or cross country. After a long debate with family and the realization I couldn't make the other teams, I was suddenly on the cross-country team. I was excited yet extremely nervous because I wasn't a runner. But I showed up at all the practices, and each day I could run farther and farther. Eventually I was out on the hilly terrain behind CSU East Bay, running with my teammates. I didn't always keep up with the pack, but I was on the team, competing and practicing with them daily.

About midway through the season, we flew to San Diego for the UCSD Triton invite. I was excited to run and see the beautiful course in San Diego. The gun went off, and everyone ran out of the gate. A mile and a half into the run, I was by myself. Everyone else was way ahead. This was a typical scene for me during cross-country season. At least I was on the team, and I was putting in the mileage. By the time I finished, most of the other teams were packing up to go home. I was embarrassed but reminded myself I had never been a runner before and had landed a spot on an NCAA cross-country team. I could have quit, but I wanted to push myself and see the results of my hard work.

The season continued, and occasionally I would end up in front of one or two other runners. Those were the days when I was really proud of my effort. At one conference league meet, we were going for the title. In cross country, the top five runners score points for the team, and there were six runners on the team. As you can imagine, I was typically the runner who never scored. The league conference title was up for grabs, and the race would be close. The course was hilly and full of twists and turns. At the start, once the gun went off, the dust flew in the air, and everyone took off with purpose. Rounding the corner with a mile to go, I looked ahead and saw one of my teammates collapsed on the side of the trail. As I approached, my coach turned his attention to me. He told me he needed me to beat the guy ahead of me to clinch the title. I was needed by the team. This lit a fire that fueled me for the rest of the race. I beat the other runner, and we won the title. We were moving on to regionals! That race was amazing and filled with such talented athletes. It was an experience I will never forget.

Cross country taught me to be humble and that I can try anything. I put myself out there to be vulnerable and embarrassed, and at the end of the day, I was an NCAA athlete. I often bring up this story with educators and students because it shows the power of moving out of your comfort zone. You don't always have to be the best; you just have to try.

Education is a team sport. We are here to support each other and do the absolute best we can for students. In order to reach the championship and see our students succeed, we must go outside our comfort zones and make things happen.

THINGS TO CONSIDER AND TWEET ————————————————

1. When was the last time you put yourself out there?
2. How do you encourage others to put themselves out there?
3. Do you share your past experiences with your students? How do they respond?

———————————————— #BETHEONE

CONNECT.

LEARN THEIR STORY.

#BETHEONE

—— 40 ——

Be the One Who Is Connected

What makes a good educator? What makes a great educator? Teaching at the elementary, middle, and high school levels has given me the opportunity to speak and build relationships with educators from all different backgrounds and walks of life. A conversation that always comes to mind is one that came while teaching at a middle school.

I was evaluated during my first year teaching middle school. While preparing for the evaluation, I kept thinking about how I really wanted to show my observer I wasn't just a good teacher; I was a *great* teacher.

During my conversation with the administrator who was evaluating me, I started talking about the different ideas I had for the department and my own teaching and pedagogy. I'm pretty passionate about kids, and once I get going, it's often hard to slow down. He finally stopped me and asked, "Where do you get all these ideas?"

With a smile, I replied, "Like all good teachers, I steal them!"

I am a huge proponent of not re-creating the wheel. Educators around the world are working tirelessly to make sure they are bringing their all, every day. Think about how much more time we would have if we all shared our resources. Being connected—from simple chats to serious networking—is vital to an educator's survival. If you haven't already, create or join a professional learning network (PLN) that will push you to become better and hold you accountable for the things you aren't doing well.

Currently, communication is always at our fingertips. No longer limited to colleagues or friends in nearby cities and states, we can communicate frequently and effectively with people all over the world.

I belong to many different PLNs that communicate via different apps. Some people find it fascinating that the relationships created within those groups are real and valued friendships, but it's true. We mentor each other, support each other, and brainstorm whenever possible.

In one of my groups, someone asked if anyone would want to present with them at a national principal's conference. I jumped at the chance because I knew it would push me beyond my comfort zone, challenge my thinking, and boost my connections. Using different avenues of communication, I met and discussed with two principals from the Midwest all about our presentation. We didn't meet in person until hours prior to the presentation, which was seamless because we were so well connected and had been building relationships for weeks.

As people seek advice on how to grow personally and professionally, I challenge them to get connected and find the game changers—both locally and globally—in their field. There are no more excuses because the technology is here, and it's easy to access. Surround yourself with people who challenge you and make you better.

THINGS TO CONSIDER AND TWEET ━━━━━━━━━━━━━━━

1. How do you connect with others?
2. What has been the biggest success that has come from connecting with other educators?
3. How do you encourage kids to get connected?

━━━━━━━━━━━━━━━━━━ **#BETHEONE**

SET THE TONE.
#BETHEONE

— 41 —
BE THE ONE WHO BLOGS

Whenever a conversation turns to blogging, my ears perk up. When people find a blog they enjoy, whether about fashion, knitting, pets, or pinching pennies, they talk about it. They like to share the ideas they're seeing with others. Most of these blogs are not written by classically trained writers but by people with passion and practical experience. These writers are excited about a hobby or profession or specific way of living, and they want to share it with the world.

When I was first encouraged to start a blog, I felt I had nothing to say. I kept thinking to myself, "I am not a writer. I am not special. No one will read it. I don't have the time." Then I realized that I had been writing my entire career—it just never took the form of blogging. Through the years, I have written articles for various education journals. It started as a way to prove something to my colleagues, who often felt I fit into that old-school coach mentality and that I was more coach than teacher. Whenever I needed some motivation, I would write. I knew few people would actually read those articles, but I loved doing it.

So I started blogging. The day of my first post, I was nervous, worried that no one would read it or find it helpful. But people did. Then I wrote another one. People kept reading. Each time I blogged, the number of readers increased. Eventually I started receiving messages thanking me for writing and sharing my thoughts. People were approaching my wife and talking about how sensitive I was.

They had never seen that side of me. Before I knew it, I had an audience, and people liked hearing the message.

Be passionate and proud, believe in your message, and make sure that's the voice that comes out through your blog. I encourage you to give it a try. You have ideas and insights many people would find interesting. You have a story unique to anyone else; no one else has seen and done the things you have done. You can even start small by blogging as a way to journal and stay motivated and inspired. The more you write, the more you will develop your own unique voice.

THINGS TO CONSIDER AND TWEET

1. If you have a blog, how has it benefitted you personally and professionally?
2. If you don't blog, why not?
3. What has been your experience with having students blog?

#BETHEONE

42

Be the One Who Creates a Student-Centered Environment

When the school year ends, educators finally have time to slow down and evaluate how things have gone that year. Most of us don't accomplish every project on our list, and we often use the summer to regroup. When the kids leave for summer, take a walk around the building, look at the walls and environment, and ask yourself one question:

Do the walls of your classroom/school/office show that you are in the business of kids?

Visiting other school sites is fun and insightful. You can pick up on the culture and climate of the school by simply walking into the office. Pictures of kids and student-centered work are often signs that the school values and environment are student centered.

Schools should be screaming that they are in the business of kids. The entire school—the hallways, the classrooms, the media center, the cafeteria, and yes, even the parking lot—should be showing these signs.

A great place to start is with your office. And not just your office, your school's front office, and every other office on campus.

Take a moment and think about your office. What does it look like? Is it a kid-centered space? What kind of art is on the walls? Is it welcoming? Is it professional?

When visitors walk into an office at your school, they should automatically smile. These offices, though certainly places where important work happens, should be welcoming, cheerful and focused on children. Too often our offices are dimly lit, cramped, and devoid of any personality.

Take time during the summer or break to give your office a makeover, and don't leave anything off the table. Think about every-thing from paint color to furniture placement to fun posters and photos. Maybe even add some kid-sized chairs to the mix! Be the One to show everyone in your community you are in the business of kids.

THINGS TO CONSIDER AND TWEET

1. What do visitors see when they walk into your school building?
2. How do you make it clear to visitors that you are in the kid business?

#BETHEONE

43

BE THE ONE WHO MAKES EDUCATION RELEVANT

When was the last time your boss asked you to do a worksheet? When was the last time your workplace gave you a project and told you to work on it all by yourself?

When was the last time your supervisor told you to create something to be used tomorrow, and thrown away in least than two months?

For most of you, the answer to each of those questions is "never." If in life we don't use these skills, why are we teaching our students to think that way?

It is time to stop thinking about how it has always been done and transform the way we teach and plan our lesson daily. Every day, stop and think about the lessons we are teaching and the skills we are developing.

Will these lessons and skills be needed in ten to fifteen years—and will they assist students in navigating the world we live in?

Do they have the critical thinking and creativity skills needed for the workforce of the future?

Walking into classrooms where the same worksheets have been passed out for decades is not challenging students to be current and future thinkers. These worksheets might be creating a base of knowledge; however, in an education system with so many possibilities, we can do better. Educators who depend on step-by-step curriculum for ideas and approaches have thrown away their creativity. Get creative and make sure your students are being set up with skills that will last a lifetime.

If done properly, project and group work allows students to learn how to interact with others and work together for a common goal. Grouping must be strategic and planned. The students must be pushed to share equally and come up with ideas then defend those ideas. Look for opportunities to group students together to work on real-life problems and have them come up with real-life solutions.

Educators, districts, and professionals are always looking at current events to make sure we are preparing our students to enter the real world. We have an obligation to our students to keep up on what is needed and look at projections for what will be needed when our kindergarteners are graduating from high school and college.

Be the One who keeps education relevant.

THINGS TO CONSIDER AND TWEET

1. How are you equipping your students for the world of tomorrow?
2. What kind of support do you need from your school district—new curriculum, equipment, learning opportunities—to make that happen?

#BETHEONE

44

BE THE ONE WHO MODELS HEALTHY LIVING

Let's say you wake up early and head to the gym in time to make it to that 5:30 a.m. spin class. In walks the teacher, overweight and still in pajamas. You probably have now lost some of your desire to be in that class, and that teacher might have lost a lot of credibility with the students and fellow staff members. It is important to remember that every day we walk into our school buildings, we are representing the education profession as a whole and have the ability to change people's perceptions for better or for worse.

As teachers, we are the face of a healthy lifestyle to our students. They look at us and see what they are trying to achieve—a healthy person with a healthy lifestyle. Being able to walk the walk and talk the talk is a big deal when it comes to our lessons, and it's just as crucial when it comes to personal appearance and behavior.

We are in such a powerful position working in the K–12 education system. Students—no matter the age—are looking to us to see what a healthy lifestyle should like. One year when I was teaching middle school physical education, we started an annual Turkey Trot. This event was a three-mile run around campus, and it would be held every period. Classroom teachers were encouraged to take their classes out to cheer on the runners. Teachers were also allowed to join in on the fun.

During fourth period, one of our school's history teachers walked up to the starting line decked out in running shoes and attire. As he approached, he claimed he was going for the victory because he wanted to win a frozen turkey to take home. That was the prize for each male and female winner of each race. Clearly skeptical, students stood there whispering their surprise, "Did you even know he could run?" The race started, and he took off with a vengeance. The leaders set the pace, and this teacher kept up. In the final fifty yards, a seventh grader passed him and won the race. But this teacher hung in there for the entire run. It was an awesome thing to see.

A few minutes later, I went looking to congratulate him and found him in the bathroom throwing up. He had pushed himself past his threshold. Eventually he recovered and even shared his embarrassment with all the students.

It wasn't until two months later that I understood the impact he'd had on our school that day. Students had been inspired by his run and his commitment to physical fitness. A running group started, and kids also started making healthier food choices. It was so refreshing, and all it took was a teacher who resolved to Be the One who models healthy living.

THINGS TO CONSIDER AND TWEET

1. How do you model healthy living for kids?
2. How do you encourage your students to be healthy?
3. What school-wide activities have you led or participated in to promote health?

#BETHEONE

— 45 —

BE THE ONE WHO MAKES KIDS WANT TO BE ON TIME

Tardiness has been an issue in schools ever since teachers started taking attendance. Some of the K–12 schools I have visited are notorious for having students show up late to class. The age-old question, "What can we do to deal with our tardy problem?" is not an easy one to answer.

We need to make students *want* to be on time. Our classes need to be so engaging, energetic, and accepting that they can't wait to get there and get started. It's no fun heading to a class about which you aren't the least bit excited. I get it. Think about yourself when you are heading to a meeting that is not engaging, energetic, or doesn't pertain to you.

HOW EXCITED ARE YOU TO BE THERE?

Do you rush in, making sure you don't miss anything?

The education system can do better. We can make kids want to be on time for class if we focus our attention on a few key areas to make sure our students want to be in class on time. Tardiness will never fix itself. We must be intentional in correcting the problem.

GREET STUDENTS AT THE DOOR.

Stand at the door of your classroom and smile at students as they arrive. Look them in the eye, shake hands, give a high-five or a fist bump—just make them feel welcome. No matter the age, students want to feel they belong in their classroom. Think of the last professional development you attended. If the presenter had stood at the door, shaking your hand and personally welcoming you to the session, I imagine it would have improved your outlook. So be aware of how you greet students—even those who are late. Welcome them with open arms, and they will be more likely to return. Greet them with sarcasm or criticism, and they will want to stay away.

KEEP THE ENERGY HIGH.

From the time students arrive at school in the morning to the moment they leave in the afternoon, we must keep the energy high. We need to be upbeat, lighthearted, and focused on having fun while learning. Kids are more perceptive than adults often give them credit for, and they pick up on bad moods, frustration, anger, and worry. When our energy is low, the climate of the classroom can change drastically.

BE UNDERSTANDING.

Life happens. As a principal, I must remember this when dealing with teachers who have conflicts arise. Once one of my teachers told me her grandfather had died and she would need a week off for his funeral. Of course, I was sympathetic and understanding. I sent the teacher on her way and lined up a substitute. Fast forward six months, and the family of a student in this teacher's class emailed her about the child needing to miss a week of school due to a death in the family. This teacher was upset and disapproved, arguing that the child would be missing a test and really could not afford to miss any more school. I was shocked. She had experienced this same situation only a few months earlier but couldn't offer the same understanding.

We must understand that all kinds of things happen in our students' lives—much of which they can't control—and we must help them navigate these twists and turns.

Be the One who understands and keeps welcoming students to the school every day. They are much more likely to be on time if they are invited and welcomed.

THINGS TO CONSIDER AND TWEET

1. How do you deal with tardiness in your classroom?
2. How are you engaging students when they walk through the door?
3. How have you seen relationships affect tardy rates?

#BETHEONE

WHAT COMPASS DO YOU USE?
#BETHEONE

46

BE THE ONE WHO CHANGES THE GAME

Starting out as a physical education teacher, I walked into my first school on the first day of the second semester. I had inherited an old-school program where not much teaching occurred. As the classes lined up and the calisthenics started, the teacher would roll out the balls. These fourth- and fifth-grade classes looked bored and knew what to expect each week because the routine never changed.

As I experienced this for the first time, I knew something needed to change. The class was not innovative or creative, allowing students to be their best. In my mind, these classes replicated the bad memories many adults have about "gym" class.

After speaking with the teacher for whom I was taking over, it was obvious he had lost his desire to be creative. I was aware this had been the pattern in the district prior to my arrival. So many regulations had been enforced that this educator felt, if he did anything outside of rolling the ball, he might face legal or professional repercussions.

Many educators across all disciplines share this view. With every new standard or restriction or new policy, some become a little less creative and a little more complacent.

So how do we change the game?

I believe we can start off by looking at how we treat each other. Every employee at our schools—clerical staff, cafeteria workers, custodians, teachers, and administrators—should be on a first-name basis. These employees should feel valued and supported in their individual jobs. When that happens, people are more likely to let their creativity flow because they trust their leaders will be on board with trying something new.

Administrators who want to work on improving the atmosphere on campus have countless options. For example, creating an opportunity for teachers to share their passions by setting aside time for a teacher showcase at staff meetings, allowing peers to learn from peers. Administrators can also roll up their sleeves, get back in the classroom, and model new lessons for teachers.

When educational institutions make it clear they welcome innovation, teachers will get the message and be more likely to change the game.

THINGS TO CONSIDER AND TWEET

1. How are you a game changer?
2. How are you changing the game daily for students?
3. If you could change anything about education, what would it be?

#BETHEONE

47

BE THE ONE WHO
STAYS FOCUSED

In the course of a school year, educators can get distracted. Something is always pulling us away from our classrooms, schools, and paperwork. During these times, it is more important than ever to focus on what's most important in education—kids!

When I was a teacher, I worked with an administrator who required everyone on her staff to turn in daily lesson plans and work until five o'clock in the evening. These lesson plans were to be very detailed and submitted a day in advance. This rule frustrated most of the teachers, who felt they were being micromanaged and forced to work outside school hours. I met with individual teachers and discussed with them how we could come together and be compliant but focus on our students. As a staff, we agreed to follow the rules and intentionally refocus on our students instead of our dissatisfaction. We resolved not to be so distracted by our daily work struggles that it affected our passion for kids.

Now that I'm a principal, I still get distracted. Calls from the central office, personnel issues, staffing needs, parent concerns, and special education are just a few of the things that occupy my mind from hour to hour on any given day. When my plate piles up, it's easy to get sucked in and spend all my time solving problems in my office. But that approach simply leads to isolation and frustration. The best way I have found to deal with mounting distractions is to get out of my office and into a classroom. Nothing helps me focus more than interacting with kids and learning alongside them. It puts a smile on my face and reminds me why I chose this profession.

We all need that little push every now and then. For years, I watched *Good Will Hunting* repeatedly. I'm not sure what it was about that movie, but it always motivated me to do better. Maybe movies aren't your thing. It could be a walk on the beach, reading a book, staring at a night sky, or knitting a scarf. I will say it generally helps to put some distance between yourself and your distractions. So do what you must to remember your passion and stay focused on what's most important.

THINGS TO CONSIDER AND TWEET

1. How do you stay focused on the right things all year long?
2. If you get caught up in the day to day, how do you refocus on the important things?

#BETHEONE

CONCLUSION

Not every educator you encounter will drop everything and try to change the life of a child. This is what turns good educators into great ones. Taking the time to build relationships with both adults and kids takes sincerity and intention. They don't just happen.

I have a very diverse educational background. Working at the elementary, middle, and high school levels with a variety of schools always left me longing for a sense of belonging. It made me want to build relationships to create the environment I wanted. I understand what children feel when they come to a new school or start the year. They share those feelings of wanting friendships, a sense of being wanted, and a place where they belong.

By no stretch of the imagination do I have everything figured out! I do understand kids, and I know that building relationships with them is the single most important thing we can do in education.

Without building those relationships, we can't lay the foundation for the necessary content to be successful. *Be the One for Kids* is much more than my stories and experiences. It is a rallying cry to all educators. We must be willing to do whatever it takes to change the life of a child.

Having dialogue with educators can unleash their power. Make sure you are surrounding yourself with people who will make you better. In return, make sure you are pushing others to be their best.

You have the power to Be the One for Kids!

INVEST IN PEOPLE.

THEY CHANGE LIVES.

#BETHEONE

Acknowledgments

I have many people to thank and acknowledge. First of all, my wife, Barbara, for believing in me and my message. She has shown the compassion and support that I needed throughout the process. To my kids: Robert, Joshua, Julianna, and Zachary for pushing me to be better each and every day.

I would not be the man I am today without my parents, Bill and Diana Sheehy. You always pushed me to be better and to shoot for the stars. To my seven siblings for showing me that life is not easy, but it is much better with a support system. To all my extended family that allows me to explore what life is all about, thank you.

I would like to thank my team at Concord High School and Highlands Elementary for challenging and inspiring me daily. Without the support of these teams, I would never have grown to where I am today.

Thank you to my PLNs for helping me grow and always being willing to pick me up on days that I need support. Thank you to my Twitter family for pushing me to be better.

Thank you to all my friends and co-educators for listening to my stories and encouraging me along the way. Thank you to Adam Welcome for believing in my message and encouraging me to share it.

Thank you to Dave and Shelley Burgess and the entire DBC team for allowing me to share my message with the world.

MORE FROM

DAVE BURGESS
Consulting, Inc.

Teach Like a PIRATE

Increase Student Engagement, Boost Your Creativity, and Transform Your Life as an Educator

By Dave Burgess (@BurgessDave)

New York Times' bestseller *Teach Like a PIRATE* sparked a worldwide educational revolution with its passionate teaching manifesto and dynamic student-engagement strategies. Translated into multiple languages, it sparks outrageously creative lessons and life-changing student experiences.

P is for PIRATE

Inspirational ABC's for Educators

By Dave and Shelley Burgess (@Burgess_Shelley)

In *P is for Pirate,* husband-and-wife team Dave and Shelley Burgess tap personal experiences of seventy educators to inspire others to create fun and exciting places to learn. It's a wealth of imaginative and creative ideas that makes learning and teaching more fulfilling than ever before.

The Innovator's Mindset

Empower Learning, Unleash Talent, and Lead a Culture of Creativity

By George Couros (@gcouros)

In *The Innovator's Mindset*, teachers and administrators discover that compliance to a scheduled curriculum hinders student innovation, critical thinking, and creativity. To become forward-thinking leaders, students must be empowered to wonder and explore.

Pure Genius

Building a Culture of Innovation and Taking 20% Time to the Next Level

By Don Wettrick (@DonWettrick)

Collaboration—with experts, students, and other educators—helps create interesting and even life-changing opportunities for learning. In *Pure Genius*, Don Wettrick inspires and equips educators with a systematic blueprint for beating classroom boredom and teaching innovation.

Learn Like a PIRATE

Empower Your Students to Collaborate, Lead, and Succeed

By Paul Solarz (@PaulSolarz)

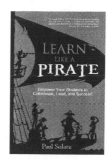

Passing grades don't equip students for life and career responsibilities. *Learn Like a PIRATE* shows how risk-taking and exploring passions in stimulating, motivating, supportive, self-directed classrooms creates students capable of making smart, responsible decisions on their own.

Ditch That Textbook

Free Your Teaching and Revolutionize Your Classroom

By Matt Miller (@jmattmiller)

Ditch That Textbook creates a support system, toolbox, and manifesto that can free teachers from outdated textbooks. Miller empowers them to untether themselves, throw out meaningless, pedestrian teaching and learning practices, and evolve and revolutionize their classrooms.

50 Things You Can Do with Google Classroom

By Alice Keeler and Libbi Miller
(@alicekeeler, @MillerLibbi)

50 Things You Can Do with Google Classroom provides a thorough overview of this GAfE app and shortens the teacher learning curve for introducing technology in the classroom. Keeler and Miller's ideas, instruction, and screenshots help teachers go digital with this powerful tool.

50 Things to Go Further with Google Classroom

A Student-Centered Approach

By Alice Keeler and Libbi Miller
(@alicekeeler, @MillerLibbi)

In *50 Things to Go Further with Google Classroom: A Student-Centered Approach*, authors and educators Alice Keeler and Libbi Miller help teachers create a digitally rich, engaging, student-centered environment that taps the power of individualized learning using Google Classroom.

140 Twitter Tips for Educators

Get Connected, Grow Your Professional Learning Network, and Reinvigorate Your Career

By Brad Currie, Billy Krakower, and Scott Rocco
(@bradmcurrie, @wkrakower, @ScottRRocco)

In *140 Twitter Tips for Educators*, #Satchat hosts and founders of Evolving Educators, Brad Currie, Billy Krakower, and Scott Rocco, offer step-by-step instruction on Twitter basics and building an online following within Twitter's vibrant network of educational professionals.

Master the Media

How Teaching Media Literacy Can Save Our Plugged-In World

By Julie Smith (@julnilsmith)

Master the Media explains media history, purpose, and messaging so teachers and parents can empower students with critical-thinking skills which lead to informed choices, the ability to differentiate between truth and lies, and discern perception from reality. Media literacy can save the world.

The Zen Teacher

Creating Focus, Simplicity, and Tranquility in the Classroom

By Dan Tricarico (@thezenteacher)

Unrushed and fully focused, teachers influence—even improve—the future when they maximize performance and improve their quality of life. In *The Zen Teacher*, Dan Tricarico offers practical, easy-to-use techniques to develop a non-religious Zen practice and thrive in the classroom.

eXPlore Like a Pirate

Gamification and Game-Inspired Course Design to Engage, Enrich, and Elevate Your Learners

By Michael Matera (@MrMatera)

Create an experiential, collaborative, and creative world with classroom game designer and educator Michael Matera's game-based learning book, *eXPlore Like a Pirate*. Matera helps teachers apply motivational gameplay techniques and enhance curriculum with gamification strategies.

Your School Rocks . . . So Tell People!

Passionately Pitch and Promote the Positives Happening on Your Campus

By Ryan McLane and Eric Lowe (@McLane_Ryan, @EricLowe21)

Your School Rocks . . . So Tell People! helps schools create effective social media communication strategies that keep students' families and the community connected to what's going on at school, offering more than seventy immediately actionable tips with easy-to-follow instructions and video tutorial links.

Play Like a Pirate

Engage Students with Toys, Games, and Comics

By Quinn Rollins (@jedikermit)

In *Play Like a Pirate*, Quinn Rollins offers practical, engaging strategies and resources that make it easy to integrate fun into your curriculum. Regardless of grade level, serious learning can be seriously fun with inspirational ideas that engage students in unforgettable ways.

The Classroom Chef

Sharpen Your Lessons. Season Your Classes. Make Math Meaningful

By John Stevens and Matt Vaudrey (@Jstevens009, @MrVaudrey)

With imagination and preparation, every teacher can be *The Classroom Chef* using John Stevens and Matt Vaudrey's secret recipes, ingredients, and tips that help students "get" math. Use ideas as-is, or tweak to create enticing educational meals that engage students.

How Much Water Do We Have?

5 Success Principles for Conquering Any Challenge and Thriving in Times of Change

By Pete Nunweiler with Kris Nunweiler

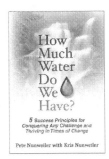

Stressed out, overwhelmed, or uncertain at work or home? It could be figurative dehydration.

How Much Water Do We Have? identifies five key elements necessary for success of any goal, life transition, or challenge. Learn to find, acquire, and use the 5 Waters of Success.

The Writing on the Classroom Wall

How Posting Your Most Passionate Beliefs about Education Can Empower Your Students, Propel Your Growth, and Lead to a Lifetime of Learning

By Steve Wyborney (@SteveWyborney)

Big ideas lead to deeper learning, but they don't have to be profound to have profound impact. Teacher Steve Wyborney explains why and how sharing ideas sharpens and refines them. It's okay if some ideas fall off the wall; what matters most is sharing and discussing.

Kids Deserve It!

Pushing Boundaries and Challenging Conventional Thinking

By Todd Nesloney and Adam Welcome (@TechNinjaTodd, @awelcome)

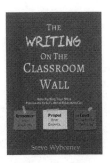

Think big. Make learning fun and meaningful. *Kids Deserve It!* Nesloney and Welcome offer high-tech, high-touch, and highly engaging practices that inspire risk-taking and shake up the status quo on behalf of your students. Rediscover why you became an educator, too!

LAUNCH

Using Design Thinking to Boost Creativity and Bring Out the Maker in Every Student

By John Spencer and A.J. Juliani (@spencerideas, @ajjuliani)

When students identify themselves as makers, inventors, and creators, they discover powerful problem-solving and critical-thinking skills. Their imaginations and creativity will shape our future. John Spencer and A.J. Juliani's *LAUNCH* process dares you to innovate and empower them.

Instant Relevance

Using Today's Experiences to Teach Tomorrow's Lessons

By Denis Sheeran (@MathDenisNJ)

Learning sticks when it's relevant to students. In *Instant Relevance,* author and keynote speaker Denis Sheeran equips you to create engaging lessons *from* experiences and events that matter to students while helping them make meaningful connections between the real world and the classroom.

Escaping the School Leader's Dunk Tank

How to Prevail When Others Want to See You Drown

By Rebecca Coda and Rick Jetter
(@RebeccaCoda, @RickJetter)

Dunk-tank situations—discrimination, bad politics, revenge, or ego-driven coworkers—can make an educator's life miserable. Coda and Jetter (dunk-tank survivors themselves) share real-life stories and insightful research to equip school leaders with tools to survive and, better yet, avoid getting "dunked."

Start. Right. Now.

Teach and Lead for Excellence

By Todd Whitaker, Jeff Zoul, and Jimmy Casas
(@ToddWhitaker, @Jeff_Zoul, @casas_jimmy)

Excellent leaders and teachers *Know the Way, Show the Way, Go the Way, and Grow Each Day.* Whitaker, Zoul, and Casas share four key behaviors of excellence from educators across the U.S. and motivate to put you on the right path.

Lead Like a PIRATE

Make School Amazing for Your Students and Staff

By Shelley Burgess and Beth Houf
(@Burgess_Shelley, @BethHouf)

Lead Like a PIRATE maps out character traits necessary to captain a school or district. You'll learn where to find treasure already in your classrooms and schools—and bring out the best in educators. Find encouragement in your relentless quest to make school amazing for everyone!

Teaching Math with Google Apps

50 G Suite Activities

By Alice Keeler and Diana Herrington

(@AliceKeeler, @mathdiana)

   Teaching Math with Google Apps meshes the easy student/teacher interaction of Google Apps with G Suite that empowers student creativity and critical thinking. Keeler and Herrington demonstrate fifty ways to bring math classes into the twenty-first century with easy-to-use technology.

Table Talk Math

A Practical Guide for Bringing Math into Everyday Conversations

By John Stevens (@Jstevens009)

   In *Table Talk Math,* John Stevens offers parents—and teachers—ideas for initiating authentic, math-based, everyday conversations that get kids to notice and pique their curiosity about the numbers, patterns, and equations in the world around them.

Shift This!

How to Implement Gradual Change for Massive Impact in Your Classroom

By Joy Kirr (@JoyKirr)

   Establishing a student-led culture focused on individual responsibility and personalized learning *is* possible, sustainable, and even easy when it happens little by little. In *Shift This!,* Joy Kirr details gradual shifts in thinking, teaching, and approach for massive impact in your classroom.

Unmapped Potential

An Educator's Guide to Lasting Change

By Julie Hasson and Missy Lennard (@PPrincipals)

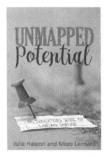

   Overwhelmed and overworked? You're not alone, but it can get better. You simply need the right map to guide you from frustrated to fulfilled. *Unmapped Potential* offers advice and practical strategies to forge a unique path to becoming the educator and *person* you want to be.

Shattering the Perfect Teacher Myth

6 Truths That Will Help You THRIVE as an Educator

By Aaron Hogan (@aaron_hogan)

Author and educator Aaron Hogan helps shatter the idyllic "perfect teacher" myth, which erodes self-confidence with unrealistic expectations and sets teachers up for failure. His book equips educators with strategies that help them shift out of survival mode and THRIVE.

Social LEADia

Moving Students from Digital Citizenship to Digital Leadership

By Jennifer Casa-Todd (@JCasaTodd)

A networked society requires students to leverage social media to connect to people, passions, and opportunities to grow and make a difference. *Social LEADia* helps shift focus at school and home from digital citizenship to digital leadership and equip students for the future.

Spark Learning

3 Keys to Embracing the Power of Student Curiosity

By Ramsey Musallam (@ramusallam)

Inspired by his popular TED Talk "3 Rules to Spark Learning," Musallam combines brain science research, proven teaching methods, and his personal story to empower you to improve your students' learning experiences by inspiring inquiry and harnessing its benefits.

Ditch That Homework

Practical Strategies to Help Make Homework Obsolete

By Matt Miller and Alice Keeler (@jmattmiller, @alicekeeler)

In *Ditch That Homework*, Miller and Keeler discuss the pros and cons of homework, why it's assigned, and what life could look like without it. They evaluate research, share parent and teacher insights, then make a convincing case for ditching it for effective and personalized learning methods.

The Four O'Clock Faculty

A Rogue Guide to Revolutionizing Professional Development

By Rich Czyz (@RACzyz)

In *The Four O'Clock Faculty*, Rich identifies ways to make professional learning meaningful, efficient, and, above all, personally relevant. It's a practical guide to revolutionize PD, revealing why some is so awful and what *you* can do to change the model for the betterment of everyone.

Culturize

Every Student. Every Day. Whatever It Takes.

By Jimmy Casas (@casas_jimmy)

Culturize dives into what it takes to cultivate a community of learners who embody innately human traits our world desperately needs—kindness, honesty, and compassion. Casas's stories reveal how "soft skills" can be honed while exceeding academic standards of twenty-first-century learning.

Code Breaker

Increase Creativity, Remix Assessment, and Develop a Class of Coder Ninjas!

By Brian Aspinall (@mraspinall)

You don't have to be a "computer geek" to use coding to turn curriculum expectations into student skills. Use *Code Breaker* to teach students how to identify problems, develop solutions, and use computational thinking to apply and demonstrate learning.

The Wild Card

7 Steps to an Educator's Creative Breakthrough

By Hope and Wade King (@hopekingteach, @wadeking7)

The Kings facilitate a creative breakthrough in the classroom with *The Wild Card*, a step-by-step guide to drawing on your authentic self to deliver your content creatively and be the *wild card* who changes the game for your learners.

Stories from Webb

The Ideas, Passions, and Convictions of a Principal and His School Family

By Todd Nesloney (@TechNinjaTodd)

    Stories from Webb goes right to the heart of education. Told by award-winning principal Todd Nesloney and his dedicated team of staff and teachers, this book reminds you why you became an educator. Relatable stories reinvigorate and may inspire you to tell your own!

The Principled Principal

10 Principles for Leading Exceptional Schools

By Jeffrey Zoul and Anthony McConnell (@Jeff_Zou, @mcconnellaw)

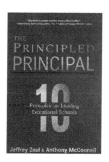

    Zoul and McConnell know from personal experience that the role of school principal is one of the most challenging *and* the most rewarding in education. Using relatable stories and real-life examples, they reveal ten core values that will empower you to work and lead with excellence.

The Limitless School

Creative Ways to Solve the Culture Puzzle

By Abe Hege and Adam Dovico (@abehege, @adamdovico)

    Being intentional about creating a positive culture is imperative for your school's success. This book identifies the nine pillars that support a positive school culture and explains how each stakeholder has a vital role to play in the work of making schools safe, inviting, and dynamic.

Google Apps for Littles

Believe They Can

By Christine Pinto and Alice Keeler (@PintoBeanz11, @alicekeeler)

    Learn how to tap into students' natural curiosity using technology. Pinto and Keeler share a wealth of innovative ways to integrate digital tools in the primary classroom to make learning engaging and relevant for even the youngest of today's twenty-first-century learners.

ABOUT THE AUTHOR

Ryan was raised in Southern California, where his diverse education experiences all started. He attended public school, private school, and was homeschooled. He has seen and been part of all types of education systems, which gives him a different perspective. Ryan is a passionate educator who has made it his mission to help everyone live up to their potential.

He also has an immense dedication to kids and to making sure all educators understand the power they have in a child's life. Ryan was a physical education teacher for ten years before taking the leap from teacher to administrator. After serving two years as a high school vice principal, Ryan is now the lead learner/principal of an elementary school in Concord, California. He prides himself on being someone who can build strong school culture, and that is exactly what has happened at the schools where he has served as an administrator.

Ryan works in the community where he lives, which allows him to build many relationships that foster a great learning environment for staff, students, and families. He also travels and speaks about creative educational practices and how we all have the power to *Be the One for Kids*. Other topics on which he speaks include Incorporating Technology, Being an Educator in Action, Creating a School Where No One Wants to Leave, and many others. He moderates a variety of Twitter chats and is very active on social media.

Ryan's wife, Barbara, and four children, Robert, Joshua, Julianna, and Zachary, are the light of his world. Ryan and his family reside in Concord, California.

CONNECT WITH RYAN

Ryansheehy.us

@sheehyrw

@sheehyrw

Made in the USA
Lexington, KY
15 May 2019